MW01245781

PRAISE FOR *MAKING A DIFFERENCE*

———————

"Small residential care homes are good for the elderly and for the bottom lines of investors, according to this insightful business study. . . . Some's expertise and passion for eldercare make her pitch all the more persuasive. An informative and business-savvy proposal for small-scale, attentive eldercare."

—Kirkus Reviews

"Nelly Some is truly a business leader in the senior care industry. Nelly's integrity, character, and tireless work ethic make her a remarkable champion and advocate for seniors."

—Leslie Anderson, co-owner of Anderson Marine
Consulting and Anderson Fisheries LLC

MAKING A DIFFERENCE

MAKING A DIFFERENCE

Investing in Better
Lives for Seniors

NELLY SOME

NS PUBLISHING

Published by NS Publishing, Renton, Washington
Makingadifferencewithnelly.com

Edited and designed by Girl Friday Productions
www.girlfridayproductions.com

Cover design: Rachel Marek
Project management: Reshma Kooner
Editorial production: Laura Dailey

ISBN (hardcover): 979-8-9902826-0-5
ISBN (paperback): 979-8-9902826-1-2
ISBN (ebook): 979-8-9902826-2-9

Library of Congress Control Number: 2024907027

First edition

INTRODUCTION

———————

Come with me on a clear day: the sun has broken through the clouds, the temperature is just right for short sleeves, and there's a soft breeze in the air. We're walking up the path to a ranch-style home, nestled in a quiet neighborhood in the outskirts of Seattle, Washington. We pass a line of well-tended, colorful flowers that frame the walkway and stand out against the manicured lawn. We've reached the door; let's open it.

"Good afternoon," an elderly, classy resident waiting for us says with a smile. She's sitting in a recliner in the living room, which is just off the entryway of the home. Her short, immaculately styled hair frames a pleasant face, and her makeup is perfectly in place. Her hands, however, are tucked beneath her.

"Good afternoon to you," we reply.

"Guess which color I have today," the senior woman says to us.

"Hmm, let me guess. Pink?"

She shakes her head no.

"Blue?"

She again moves her head to indicate the negative. We may be wondering what this conversation is all about, but before we ask, she pulls her hands out from beneath her. Then she holds them up daintily, show-ing off her fingernails for us to see.

They are painted a delicate lilac color, and the polish looks fresh.

"Oh, I love them," I say. "They are cuter than mine."

She smiles again, probably to agree with the statement. But her face reflects genuine pleasure.

"The salon lady came yesterday, right on time as always, to paint my nails," she says.

This incident may seem like a minor event, but it's worth noting the context to give you a full picture. This scene has been played out, time and again, at one of the residential care homes I built from the heart. It's a conversation I've had, week after week, with a satisfied resident. This elderly woman used to have her nails done regularly when she lived on her own. Ever since she was young, she's valued class and style and loved to look fresh.

Like many seniors, she always treasured her independence, but she reached the point when she needed some help to get around every day. Her family looked for a place where she could find the right kind of care. Imagine if they had put her in a different place. They could have cho-sen a nursing home with a high concentration of residents who lacked consistent personalized care, or an assisted-living center that offered ser-vices in a uniform way to all its residents. Other large-scale retirement communities might not have provided exactly what she wanted. (While some of these facilities may be great, the reality is that you have to find the right one! And it's not always easy.) She may have had to give up some of those things she loved, like getting her nails done every week by a professional.

But she didn't go to an overcrowded place where she might run the risk of becoming just a number. Instead, her family brought her to one of my care homes, where she went through the same process as all our incoming residents. This involves a series of questions to learn what they like to do, what their hobbies are, and other details about their daily lives. We're not trying to be intrusive. Quite the opposite: we care about these seniors as individuals and want to learn what they like so we can provide it for them. While larger facilities often provide a thorough questionnaire for new residents too, it's not always possible for these places to execute a customized plan. That's why I founded this type of personalized senior home. I made a model that can truly cater to older people's needs and make their experience fulfilling.

I'm driven to help the elderly population, and I understand that this kind of high-quality care starts by sitting down and getting to know the individual and their family. In the example of the elderly woman with the cute nails, she told us she had always had regular manicures in the past. She expressed interest in continuing that tradition. Of course, we can do that in the homes I've established. These are small homes, which have a maximum of six to ten elderly residents living in them, so we can prioritize their interests and make sure this type of request is met. It may seem like a small thing, but it's really a big deal.

You can tell from the smile on my elderly friend's face when she greets you that she's loving it. Just having those nails painted might be the only thing she looks forward to all week. By seeing a nail-salon professional and getting that regular manicure, she feels like she is still maintaining her lifestyle. Plus, she looks super stylish and we have fun bantering about her latest color.

That's important to me. That exact smile is at the core of why I started a residential care business. It stems from my desire to create a caring, loving home for seniors who need assistance in their daily activities. To me, it's more than dishing up breakfast for them, doling out their medications, and tucking them in at night. Over the years, I've realized that giving all seniors a sense of independence despite their needs and health conditions, such as dementia, is very therapeutic. This includes activities they can control on their own, like how their nails are painted. You'd be surprised to see just how much frustration and stress is alleviated by giving them that sense of independence. It is, essentially, providing them with a little of their old life that they can hang on to. It's about respecting who they were before and encouraging them to do things that allow them to feel like that person.

And guess what? As I've learned, the better you treat people, the more comes back to you, both in the satisfaction you get for doing the right thing and also in terms of having a successful business. I gathered all my good ideas gleaned from twenty years of experience and put them to work in these residential care homes. I successfully implemented a variety of innovations and resident-focused techniques for managing them. And as a result, the seniors are thriving. Furthermore, the families we serve are happier and more than willing to pay for this amazing peace of mind.

Investing in this type of home environment, then, helps seniors live their best lives and also provides a great return. I've seen these rewards in action throughout the years I've been involved in this business. When we care for the elderly as family, we get to see how we are making a difference, every day. I always explain to caregivers, providers, and investors that they are helping to improve the quality of life provided to the aging segment of society. Caregivers get the special chance to build a relationship with an older person and learn from them. Others involved can be assured that they are playing a role in a model I created specifically to enable older folks to live their lives to the fullest.

I didn't just come up with these ideas out of the blue or have an epiphany when I was out for an evening walk. I developed an entire system, which includes this sense of caregiving with heart, during my years of working in the eldercare industry. I've spent more than two decades caring for seniors professionally, working my way up from the ground level. I've worked in nearly every aspect of eldercare, from hospitals to nursing homes and assisted-living facilities. Along the way, I saw what was done well and what wasn't.

And trust me, I saw a lot of things that were wrong. I always promised myself that I would make them right when I had a chance.

But before we get to that, let's back up a little more. This story of caring for the elderly, truly making their environment a place where they feel well loved and provided for, goes back to a different place and time. To Africa, actually. And my birth. Let me explain . . .

I was born in Kenya and, at the age of two weeks, given to my grandmom. She raised me from infancy into adulthood, and for most of those years, it was just the two of us under one roof. She was already elderly when I entered her life, and I always had a great deal of love and respect for her. I could see what she did to take care of me and raise me. She made homemade meals, cooking everything from scratch. She showed me how to work hard, how to take care of myself, how to save money, and, most importantly, how to love and respect all human beings, regardless of their circumstances. Since it was just the two of us, I learned to be a survivor at an early age.

In our household, money wasn't in abundance in those days. When I was five years old and going to school, I would use my breaks from classes to look for ways to make a little more money and help support Grandmom. While other children played after classes, I would leave school, which was located in town, and head out a little way into the countryside. There I would buy vegetables from the farmers who grew them. I would divide up those vegetables and take them to the city, where I would sell them for a little profit.

Grandmom, in turn, showed me how to tuck away the money I made from that job, along with others I had during my younger years. With every opportunity, I worked to support our little family. Grandmom encouraged me to keep saving for college, so I did.

During those early years, Grandmom did all she could to take care of me. Since she was older and not in prime health, she got sick—a lot. When I was a little kid, I would go fetch water for her if she was ill. I would run to the neighbor's for help if she needed something that I couldn't easily get for her when she was in bed. I ran errands and prepared meals for her. I made the food from scratch, just like she had taught me. In this way, I learned to be responsible at a very early stage in life.

Those lessons in responsibility helped me put myself through college in Kenya. And the close relationship I had with my grandmom made me want to continue helping others. Caring for those in need seemed to be in my DNA. I was always looking for ways to make things easier for people.

To that end, I got a degree in tourism so I could help show people around the country. But I didn't just spend my days pointing out lions and elephants on safaris to those with flashing cameras. I also took on social causes, working as a paralegal for an organization that provided help to both AIDS patients and AIDS orphans, as well as tending to women who were victims of domestic violence and discrimination. This idea of helping others was simply ingrained in me, and when asked to help, I always said yes. Then I listened to people to really understand the problem, get to know them, and work with them to find the best solution.

After finishing school and working for some time in Africa, I came to America looking to continue building my life. I didn't have a job, but I did have a background in tourism and working for social causes. When the plane landed in the state of Washington, I didn't see any lions or elephants! Given that, I knew I would go in a different direction from tourism.

There was more to it than that, however. I knew, deep down, that I wanted to help with the elderly and care for the older generation. Doing so was naturally part of who I was, as I had already spent my lifetime looking after my grandmom. My years with her had instilled in me both a reverent respect for the older generation and a lifelong desire to help everyone in that age group.

As I settled in the Seattle metro area, I found myself thousands of miles from her, in a new country, and I really missed her. Looking out for others like Grandmom would be a way for me to help fill that void and continually feel connected to her. A concern for the elderly would drive me to work hard and find the best way to care for them with my resources and knowledge.

Even though I knew I wanted to be involved in eldercare, getting a job wasn't a simple thing. The degree I had received in Kenya wasn't widely recognized, and when I asked about transferring credits, I was told I would have to start with a class that taught English as a second language. I felt like I was going through elementary school again, starting with first grade.

Since I had to start from scratch, I decided to go back to school and study in the medical field. I took on multiple jobs—sometimes managing between five and six—to make ends meet while I finished a new degree. Some of these first odd jobs included working in the library and sorting mail in a post office. I drew from my grandmom's teachings on how to be responsible, how to be wise with money, and how to work hard to survive during those years.

I eventually got a job that lined up with my interest in eldercare. Starting at the ground level, I worked as a certified nursing assistant in a hospital. I thought it would be a good chance to get to know the industry and healthcare systems in America. I was thrilled to be placed in a unit that had senior patients.

However, I saw so many things there that just weren't correct. I could see that these senior patients were facing the end of their lives and often felt like they were losing their sense of independence because of how they were being treated. Rather than living by themselves in their own homes, they were in hospital beds and had to eat at precise times, sometimes being served food they didn't care for or want, unable to pursue the activities they used to love and do often. I tended to them as best as I could, but my heart ached for the conditions I frequently saw. "This isn't how my grandmom would want to be treated," I would think.

I also worked in assisted-living centers, often tending to between nineteen and twenty-four residents at a time during a shift. I knew the older people living at these care centers were there to get help, and I wanted to make sure they were given the assistance they needed, plus a high quality of life. I'm naturally chatty, and I loved to stay and talk to my elderly patients. I would sit down with a resident during my shift and get to know them. I could tell they were really happy to have that chance to talk. They were used to caregivers who followed the system and went through the motions, then left without having a real conversation. I didn't. I stayed.

And as we conversed, their faces would light up. I would ask about their pasts, and they would share some of their experiences with me. By learning about them, I figured I could understand their preferences and try to help them more.

But really, there was practically no time for chitchat. You see, I had to care for so many patients during a single shift, and the clock kept ticking. While I was overseeing these residents, each one had to be fed, bathed, given medication, and so on. There was a long checklist that each caregiver received, and we had to go through each item and make sure it was done.

Going through the tasks didn't bother me. My issue was that there weren't enough minutes in the day to account for social interaction with the residents. You really couldn't develop a one-on-one relationship with your patients. The job consisted mostly of just checking off those tasks listed for the day. As much as I wanted to have a close relationship with each of my senior patients, extra time simply wasn't built into the system, and that bothered me a lot.

The nursing homes I worked in were not much better. In these facilities, it often appeared at first glance that there were plenty of opportunities for senior residents to socialize and carry out independent activities. If family members were looking for a place to bring their parent or loved one and opted to take a tour, they would probably be impressed. They would see activity rooms, therapy areas, and places where seniors could exercise within the facility.

But the way their loved one would live day-to-day would not always coincide with this initial picture. Think of it like this: Let's say that in a general nursing facility, there are a hundred resident patients. Each of them has a different personality with different care needs. One has dementia, one has Parkinson's disease, and so on. Many of them have a combination of health conditions, and each one of them likely has their own unique preferences for the activities they want to do and when they want to do them.

Now you need to accommodate exercises and therapies for all of them. The care facility will come up with a care plan for each resident. Then it's the job of the caregiver to see that this care plan is followed. But it's not a tailor-made solution. For instance, the meals may be mass-produced, but the individual needs a special diet. Nutritionally speaking, the resident receives what is outlined in the care plan. The actual meal, however, might include a vegetable or dish the senior doesn't care for or hasn't eaten in years. The resident may choose not to eat it and, in doing so, miss out on the opportunity to get a nutritious meal. (Please keep in mind that I am not suggesting *all* nursing homes are like this! But I have found that many struggle to provide individualized care; they simply can't make it work in their business model, which already includes massive overhead and medical-staff costs to look after so many residents. That's why personalized, customized care has significant advantages, if the family can make it work.)

"There has to be a better way," I thought. While I was working as a caregiver in these larger settings, a friend told me of a different option. It was a residential care home, designed to accommodate a very small number of people, generally as few as six to eight. In Washington, this type of home is called an adult family home. In other areas of the country, you'll hear it referred to as residential assisted living or a senior-care group home. In this book, we'll call it a residential care home. In these types of settings, caregivers are provided around the clock, and residents are able to live in a homelike environment, with all their daily needs, from laundry to exercise to meals and medication, fully met.

It was easy to see why the level of care improved in these homes. There wasn't as much pressure to complete long lists of tasks for so many residents, and caregivers could therefore take more time to see how the residents wanted to spend their days. Certainly, all tasks still had to be completed, but there was more time available to do other very important things, like chat and interact with the seniors. Better yet, there was a high level of flexibility, so if a resident didn't want to have breakfast at a certain time, it was easier to push the time back or move it forward.

So, after working as a certified nursing assistant in hospitals, assisted-living facilities, and nursing homes and as a private caregiver, I was thrilled to eventually start working in and managing residential care homes. Even as I worked my way up, I could see there was still room for improvement. In the homes I managed, I often had ideas for ways to make the places even better for the residents. For example, I was always thinking about how the home could not only provide great care but also look like a place that someone would be really proud of. Sometimes those ideas could be implemented, but other times, since I wasn't the owner of the residential care business, I wasn't able to put a new policy in place that would really help the seniors. This kept me thinking!

During this time, I decided to become involved with real estate as a complementary business and oversaw the sale of many homes. I even purchased some myself, fixed them up, and sold them. This experience, along with what I had seen in residential care homes, made me wonder: What if I put everything together? What if I purchased a house and made it into my own residential care home?

That was exactly what I did. Starting with an initial home, I set it up and poured everything I had learned along the way into it. I drew on my experiences with my grandmom and the inherent admiration I have always had for the elderly and set policies accordingly. I was excited about the chance to really change the way older adults could live. I was also motivated to create an atmosphere that didn't include some of the mistakes and nonpersonalized policies I had seen during my earlier care-giving days at eldercare institutions.

As a result, I built a home where residents thrived. It wasn't just me who saw it. My homes filled up—fast. I had family members walk in and start crying because they were so overjoyed to see their loved one doing so well under my care. Others who owned residential care homes came to me and asked, "How do you do it? How are your homes so well liked and received by the people in them and their families?"

I was quick to share some of the steps; at the same time, I also set about expanding the business. I wanted to help more people, and so I created more residential care homes. Since I owned them, I could set my own policies and craft a culture that really sought to treat every resident like family. Over time, I built and managed many of these businesses.

What surprised me was that this residential care home model I had created did more than make our residents happy. It was actually a great business venture. Here we were, doing all we could to honor people like my grandmom every day, treating our residents like our own dearly loved family members and letting them get their nails done when they wanted. And business was booming. This social good—to help the elderly—had turned into a lucrative source of revenue.

Furthermore, the more people who contributed to this type of business, the more residents we could help. Bringing in more investors would create a winning situation for everyone involved. We could develop more resident-focused care homes, which would allow a growing number of America's aging population to get high-quality care. At the same time, investors in these homes would have the chance to tap a market with significant, continuous returns. Managers and caregivers would have the opportunity to earn a steady paycheck in a fulfilling career. They could work in a positive atmosphere and feel confident that they were contributing to a good cause.

I want to note that setting up a residential care home isn't as easy as putting up a sign and opening the doors. There's an immense amount of work involved to get it started. You have to meet a long list of regulations before you even accept residents. After that, you have to maintain your licenses to remain open.

Even when a home follows these guidelines, it might still falter. I've seen many close their doors after several years. They might have to shut down because they didn't stay on top of their licensing requirements, or they didn't hire the right caregivers, or they didn't establish a caring culture.

That's why my homes have consistently shone above the others. I have always strived for my homes to follow the licensing laws that are in place. I have aimed to thoroughly screen and get to know new caregivers before hiring them. I've worked to provide incentives for these caregivers to stay, and I offer high-quality care, train them to follow the thoughtful policies I have put in place, and continually look for ways to make the residential home experience even more personal.

What I've developed is a model that helps seniors in a loving way and provides high cash flow at the same time. It means giving more to people and having more flow back to you. The system creates advantages and a personal satisfaction for seniors, caregivers, managers, and investors.

In the following pages, we'll look at the need for these residential care homes. We'll study the aging population and see why today is an opportune time to jump into this type of investment and business. We'll go through the rigorous process of setting up a home and making sure it meets all the requirements. Then we'll walk through best practices that make these homes stand out and bring in more residents. By the end of this book, you'll be ready to call me to get involved. Let me assure you, there's something for everyone in this model, from investors to supervisors and caregivers! Read on to see the rewards unfold, and when you reach out to get started, I'll be ready and waiting.

CHAPTER 1

———

Common Types of Housing for America's Aging Population

If you are looking to make a difference—a real difference—in the lives of not just one person but several, or a dozen, or even hundreds or more, read on. I'm going to show you why investing in a residential care home is about showing love to seniors. Let's face it: these older folks need to feel wanted and to have an enjoyable place where they can spend their retirement years.

And my residential care homes have always provided that kind of great experience. I used methods that encouraged residents to be happy in the first places I managed. As I've expanded the business to include more homes, investors, providers, and caregivers, that mission remains. Being involved in my system is really about playing a role in a venture filled with heart. To understand where I'm coming from and how this works, let's return once again to my homeland of Africa. Specifically, to Kenya.

When I was growing up in Kenya, it was natural for me to have an elderly person at home. After all, my grandmom raised me. She had been part of my life since I could first remember, an essential family member who brought me up and helped me grow into an adult. I couldn't imagine my life without her.

Perhaps my upbringing wasn't exactly like everyone else's. I understand that we are all different and that our early years tend to be diverse, depending on who makes up our family and what their values are. One thing, however, is certain: we all share an understanding that there is an elderly population. Even if your grandfather didn't live with you at home, maybe you visited him when you were little. Or perhaps you see older people when you go to the grocery store. News programs and television shows often feature the previous generation. In short, we know they're around.

The reason I bring up this recognition of the elderly in our lives is to point out that this segment of the population is very real. Older people might look frail on the outside, but they have extensive pasts. They have their own preferences, likes and dislikes. Moreover, the majority of them, like my grandmom, spent many years waking up, living day after day, and going to sleep inside a comfortable home.

And that's where they want to stay.

While aging in place—a housing option we'll look at in a little more depth momentarily—tends to be what our grandparents, parents, and loved ones prefer, we all know that they usually can't live independently forever. Time ticks on, and age-related conditions set in. When I think of my grandmom, I see a woman with a sharp mind but a slowing body. As the years passed, she, like many others, needed to rely on some form of help to go about her day.

This shift—from living at home to needing help during the senior years—is happening in homes throughout society. Think of a nice, recently retired couple in their sixties who live down the street. You see them drive their car around and go out for walks in the evening. They always smile and wave or chat when you cross paths.

But what happens when that older couple ages ten more years? Or what if we fast-forward fifteen or even twenty years? When that same elderly couple reaches their eighties, they might still be driving and walking. They may not, however, be able to do as many things as they once did. They may have someone come in and clean their house every week, a chore they used to take care of on their own. Over time, they could slowly pass on more duties to other, younger, healthier folks who are willing to lend them a hand.

Or the husband might suddenly have a heart attack one day. In an instant, their peaceful life in the suburbs ends. This medical crisis will forever alter their lives. Think screaming sirens as they race to the emergency room, a long hospital stay, and then . . . a doctor walking in and announcing that they can't return home. The wife isn't strong enough to take care of the husband, and the husband isn't well enough to be on his own. All at once, they might need to seek more healthcare or move to a different place. It's a shocking, traumatic shift for both of them.

This, in a nutshell, is a commonsense look at the process of aging. For our discussion, it's important to remember that these scenes are happening all the time. It is estimated that in the United States, the number of people who are sixty-five years old or older will reach ninety-five million in 2060. Compare that to 2018, when the size of the sixty-five-and-older age group was just fifty-two million.[1] That amounts to nearly double the number of seniors walking around—and going through health transitions—in just a few decades.

Needless to say, these older folks are going to play a larger role in our lives. And you may already know elderly people in your own neighborhood or family or friend circle, who are going through aging transitions. What are some common issues you hear about these individuals? If they're like my grandmom, they may have certain health complications, meaning they aren't as spry and active as they once were. They may be full of knowledge and have interesting experiences to share, based on the decades they've been on this earth and the different periods they've lived through. Some may have seen World War II or been a part of a later war; others might have lived through tough economic times or grown up in booming societies. All of them have witnessed changes in technology and watched the world become more digital. They've observed the dial-up phone, its cord connected to the kitchen wall, get sideswiped by the smartphone. They remember the days of older cars, differently styled homes, and various bygone fashion trends. In other words, they have lived. Really lived.

And now they keep on their paths of life. Where will these folks carry out their daily routines, and what will they do as they grow older? This is a key question and one that many will ask at some point in their lives. In some countries, it's accepted that the elderly will live with their families and the younger generation will take care of them. For the purpose of our conversation, let's look at caregiving services in the United States and lay out some of the common housing situations typically available to the older generation.

AGING IN PLACE

This is when an older person wants to remain at home for as long as possible. Aging in place is, hands down, what most seniors in the United States want to do. When I mentioned this earlier, I wasn't kidding. The American Association of Retired Persons (AARP) backs up my hunch. According to their data, nearly 90 percent of people over the age of sixty-five want to stay in their homes for as long as possible.[2]

Such a large percentage of Americans prefer to live in their own place that it's likely you've crossed paths with someone who wears those aging-in-place shoes. Maybe it's your mom, your dad, or an older aunt. Perhaps it's a grandparent or mentor who has been in your life for a long time. Ask them why they want to stay at home, and they might just shrug and say, "Because I have always been here."

Dig a little deeper, however, and you'll find many underlying psychological reasons that explain why they want to age in place. And while the exact motivations to stay at home will be as varied as the individuals themselves (after all, we are all unique), there are some common ones that are worth pointing out. First, many people just want to keep doing what they have always done. They might have lived on their own, independently, for the past fifty or sixty years. That's a long time.

And they may be very used to living in their current place. Perhaps they built their dream home, or their forever home, in their forties, fifties, or sixties. They then spent the next decades living in it, creating traditions and carrying them out, year after year. Visitors and family members dropped in, stayed, and left their marks within those walls. The seniors may have decorated the house a certain way for the holidays, cut the lawn the same way every week, or played cards with the same group of friends once a month.

All those memories, along with routines that come with everyday life, mean that the place where the elderly live during their retirement is inherently special to them. They know where the kitchen is, how the living room is arranged, how to turn on the TV, and where to find their favorite chair on the porch. These things might seem frivolous or obvious, but stop and think about it. As people grow older, they tend to like things how they are. There's often a reason for that. It might be harder to move around, for one. If it's tough to put one foot in front of the other or to get out the cane and take some steps, it's nice to know where you're going and when you'll arrive. For someone seventy or eighty years old, those movements and steps become even more purposeful.

Another reason why older folks like to stay right where they are stems from the phrase "There's no place like home." Consider that statement for a moment. If elderly individuals feel strongly that they want to be in their own house that also means they likely have a set opinion about change. In short, they don't want it.

Consider what moving implies for an older person, based on what we just established as our natural affinity for a comfortable, familiar setting. To simply leave behind a place that might have boxes and boxes filled with memories from the past twenty to sixty years or more? It's not so easy. At an older age, you don't usually just pack up and move to a new place. You also don't usually volunteer to go through the hassle of sorting keepsakes, lining up movers, and picking out a home with a different kitchen, or a tiny living room, or no porch on which to put your favorite chair.

Elderly folks fear losing their independence when they think about leaving their home. Staying where they are helps them feel empowered and more like they are in control of their lives. They might like going to the grocery store on their own, visiting friends when they want to, driving to restaurants for a dinner out, or catching a movie whenever they are in the mood. They likely have established routines and ways of doing things that make them feel comfortable. An elderly person might get up early every day and have a breakfast of coffee, toast, and juice while watching the sun rise. Or they might like putting their feet up and watching the news at the same time each evening. These little rituals are often the most important to a person as they age, and they will want to hang on to them for as long as possible.

Finally, the fear of the unknown is a strong reason why the majority of elderly folks want to stay right where they are. They know about the creaking window at night; they know just how to adjust the thermostat so that they are warm but not too hot during the day, and they know when to check the mail. Moving to a new place can seem foreign and unsafe.

While most seniors understandably want to stay at home, it's not always simple to do that. Only 43 percent of people over the age of seventy say that living on their own is "very easy," according to the AARP.[3] Medical conditions, changes in their mental capacity, and just plain growing older can all lead to the need for more care.

In response to this, in recent years, it has become more common to modify homes and bring in some help on a regular basis. For example, a person who finds it a little hard to move around in the bathroom might put in grab bars on the wall. Or their family members might take out a regular tub and put in a walk-in shower so that they don't have to worry about taking a big step when it's time to bathe. Also, seniors might have a healthcare aide come in once a week to check their blood pressure, make sure they are taking their medications, and monitor a chronic condition like diabetes or heart disease. A home-care service may send a person every week to bring in some prepared meals so the senior doesn't have to worry about cooking every night.

All these things enable an older person to stay in their home for as long as possible. There often comes a point, however, when living at home—even with some form of help—just isn't possible anymore. This brings us to our next set of options, which are what seniors who need more care or their families will often consider. We'll go over a basic definition of each choice, and then look at some of the advantages and potential drawbacks of each one.

ASSISTED LIVING

Assisted-living housing is pretty much what it sounds like. The idea is to provide some form of help or assistance so a senior can continue living somewhat independently. That said, the way that assisted living is carried out can vary from state to state. Every place tends to set its own regulations and standards for this type of care.

Given this, we'll go over a general version of assisted living to understand what it typically involves. Assisted-living facilities are usually buildings that house a large number of seniors. They typically have between 25 and 120 (sometimes more) beds in them,[4] along with staff who help take care of the seniors. In the United States, a resident usually pays an average of $4,000 a month to stay in an assisted-living facility.[5]

Assisted-living facilities are usually set up in a way that provides the senior some personal space and also includes areas where they can be with others. For instance, a facility might offer a senior their own private bedroom and bathroom. The senior might also have a mini kitchen and living-room area for their own personal use. In some settings, this arrangement is kind of like having their own small apartment. The building will also have common areas, like a cafeteria where residents can eat their meals or an exercise room where seniors can go to get some activity.

Since the residents in an assisted-living facility usually need higher levels of care than what they can manage at home, the place will generally provide their meals for them. Staff members might come and help them go to the bathroom once during the night or stop in every morning to give them their medication and the day's meals. Assisted-living facilities usually provide transportation to other places, so if a resident needs to go to the doctor or run an errand, a little van or minibus might take them to their appointment or a shopping center and then bring them back to the facility.

Assisted-living places also typically provide twenty-four-hour support and access to care. If an emergency happens, there's a medical team to deal with the health crisis or take the resident to the emergency room or hospital. The ongoing healthcare support is a big reason why a family might look into this option for their loved one. They want to think that their aging parent or relative will have around-the-clock monitoring and help if any is needed. A family might also choose this option if they are trying to take care of an aging parent on their own and feel like, from a medical point of view, they just can't do it anymore.

For their residents, assisted-living facilities often make up a care plan. This means they look at what an individual needs for aspects such as their diet, medication, exercise, and therapies. Based on this plan, they create a chart that shows what the senior needs to do every day. Staff members receive the chart and check off the activities and tasks as they are carried out.

One bit of caution here: Due to their size and the number of residents within their walls, assisted-living centers often run the risk of not providing personalized attention. The ratio of staff members to residents might be something like one to ten or one to twenty, meaning a caregiver has to oversee ten or twenty patients during their shift. And while most staff members have big hearts and want to help older people, these same caregivers might have so many boxes to check on those detailed charts during their working hours that it is hard to really get to know the seniors and help them in a one-to-one way.

Another possible drawback is that an assisted-living facility is, by and large, only a temporary solution. The place is set up to support elderly folks who can mostly live independently but need some help. If (and usually when) the time comes when a senior needs more aid than the facility can provide, they will have to be moved to a different place that has more medical care, like a nursing home. Families are often surprised by this, as they may think that by placing their loved one in an assisted-living facility, they are setting up a permanent solution. Imagine their surprise when they get a call informing them their relative had to be taken to the hospital and can't return to the assisted-living facility because the place isn't equipped for the medical care the senior's new condition requires.

NURSING HOMES

Seniors typically "land" in nursing homes in two ways. They might live at home but then have an injury that leads them to a hospital and, later, to a nursing home for rehab care. Or they may live at home, move to an assisted-living facility to get more help, and then have an accident or medical emergency that takes them to the hospital and on to the nursing home for higher levels of medical care.

In terms of the level of care provided, this option includes more health surveillance than assisted living. Nursing homes usually provide as many services as seniors can get without actually being admitted to a hospital.[6] Think of a nursing home as a long-stay hospital. These facilities will look different from place to place; however, their guidelines and regulations are generally similar. That said, it's worth noting that nursing homes tend to be more highly regulated than assisted-living centers.[7]

Some nursing homes are the spitting image of a hospital. They have beds in rooms where the patients stay and nursing stations on each floor. Certain nursing homes offer private rooms, and others will also have specialized units, like a memory-care area for residents with Alzheimer's or dementia.[8]

In general terms, nursing homes give twenty-four-hour help. They usually focus on skilled-nursing-care services. Skilled nursing refers to care that is medically necessary and can only be carried out by people with the right training and licenses.[9] It's typically more costly than assisted living.

If you walk through the halls of a nursing home, you might see nurses tending to patients. You could also observe therapists helping residents. If you're handed information about what a nursing home provides, you might see terms like *orthopedic services, breathing treatments, support services for post-surgery,* and *wound care.* Most nursing homes have nutritional counseling, social work services, recreational activities, and hospice care.[10] The national average cost for a private room in a nursing home is much higher than that for assisted living.[11]

Staying in a nursing home, then, might be viewed as a solution for those who need ongoing help to get through the day and night. Family members could consider this option if a senior has just had surgery and needs some time to recover. Older folks who can't get out of bed or who have severe cognitive conditions might also turn to a nursing home for ongoing care.

If you take a tour of a nursing home, you'll usually see beds filled with people who have significant health challenges. More than 80 percent of nursing-home residents need help with at least three regular daily tasks, like dressing or bathing. Approximately 90 percent look for aid when they walk. And cognitive conditions are common in nursing homes. Between 50 and 70 percent of residents typically struggle with dementia, and two-thirds of residents have memory issues.[12]

I would be remiss not to pause and point out a key disadvantage of some nursing homes. In these places, you might find an atmosphere that feels like a medical institution. By and large, that's because the facility houses a large number of residents. It's not uncommon to find between 100 and 150 elderly folks living in a nursing home. You might have one caregiver looking after fifteen or twenty residents during their shift. The nursing home, to be profitable, might not be able to take on any more caregivers. Or they may not want to, because they are focusing on bringing in as much revenue as possible and covering other costs.

Finances aside, step back with me for a minute and ponder that ratio we just mentioned. Imagine you're a caregiver. You're one person, running around, giving breakfast trays to eighteen people during your shift. Then you might have to help them dress and clean themselves, and make sure they get to the bathroom. And that's just the start of your list. Where is the time to see how Mrs. Jones is doing today? You guessed it. There usually isn't any. Your minutes are consumed with passing out those trays of eggs and hash browns, putting toothpaste on toothbrushes, changing bedding, and on and on. There's no box to check on that long task list to tell you what questions to ask Mrs. Jones to learn who she is as a human being. There are no information packets that explain the benefits Mrs. Jones will have if you sit down and spend a few minutes with her to find out how she is doing and get to know her better.

As you can see, nursing homes, like assisted-living facilities, are sometimes set up to operate more as systems and institutions than small, homely environments. In either place, it wouldn't be unusual to find a harried caregiver racing around trying to tend to all the residents the system has placed on their plate. The care facilities are designed to deal with large numbers. Given this, caregivers often just don't have the time to really understand who the seniors are as individuals. In the end, residents can feel left alone and on their own.

CONTINUING-CARE RETIREMENT COMMUNITY (CCRC) OR MEMORY-CARE FACILITIES

You may have also encountered another type of living arrangement that provides several housing options for seniors on one campus. It is often referred to as a continuing-care retirement community (CCRC) or memory-care facility. In these places, seniors might start living in small apartments on their own. Then, when they need more help, they might move to the on-site assisted-living facility. And if they reach the point when they need ongoing care, they will go to—you guessed it—the on-site nursing home. It's sort of an all-in-one deal.

Before continuing, we should note that, like the other options, a CCRC or memory-care facility can be set up in a number of ways. The independent apartments might be small, for instance, or they might be on the larger side; meanwhile, the community itself might sit on a large property with several buildings or on a smaller property with everything close together, or perhaps have some other arrangement. Typically, however, all three living options—independent housing, assisted living, and a nursing facility—are available in just one community.

"Who goes there?" you ask. Well, some folks might choose a CCRC or a memory-care facility if they are able to live on their own now but know that they'll soon need help. A couple could also opt to go there, especially if one person requires an extra helping hand. Say the spouse who needs more help has severe memory problems. Maybe they choose a CCRC or memory-care facility so that they have some options available if the healthy spouse has to get more care in the future.

While this might initially sound like a sort of winning buffet option (everything you want in one place), it's important to point out that these communities aren't for everyone. Not all cities and counties offer this option, for one, so it's not as easy to find a CCRC or memory-care facility as it is to locate other types of care. Also, they are usually a high-fee choice. If you want to move into one, just getting in is sort of like buying a new house—a big one, that is—in terms of the financial commitment. Residents might have to shell out six figures or more as an entrance fee.[13] And it doesn't stop there. Then they have to pay a monthly fee, and this can go up when more care is needed.[14]

In summary, it's easy to understand why most seniors want to stay at home as long as possible. For those who can no longer live on their own, having a place that feels comfortable and meets their needs is important. I've explained how assisted-living facilities can help seniors maintain some level of independence; however, they typically have larger numbers of residents and are usually only a temporary solution. Nursing homes provide more medical services than assisted-living facilities and tend to be pricier. They can also feel like an institution, and seniors may find they lack personalized attention. CCRCs and memory-care facilities typically offer several levels of care for older folks, including independent living, assisted living, and nursing-home care. However, they come with high costs, and you won't find these places everywhere. They are only in certain cities and states and not as widespread as assisted-living facilities and nursing homes.

Faced with all these options, it can be tough for families to sort through the choices they have for their aging loved ones. It's not always easy to find a perfect spot in a location that relatives can regularly visit. And the search is often stressful for everyone involved.

This is precisely why I decided to open residential care homes that help seniors find a great place where they have the opportunity to be happy. In the next chapter, we'll take a closer look at these residential care businesses I've developed. I'll explain the priorities I set for these homes. I'll also compare this model to other senior living options. Let's move on and see what residential care homes have to offer.

CHAPTER 2

————

The Concept of My Residential Care Home Model

While we'll look closely at residential care homes and how they work in detail in the next chapters, I want to pause here and share an overview so we can compare it to other senior-housing options. Here it's important to keep in mind that not all types of residential care homes are the same. The exact setup will depend on the regulations of the state where the home is located. It will also vary because different managers and providers run their homes in distinct ways.

Speaking in a general sense, then, we can say that a residential care home is a family home that serves a small number of seniors. It's sort of a step up, in terms of care, from living on your own, but it is not as institutional as a nursing home. Seniors who live at a residential care home usually need some help getting through their day and may have extensive medical needs, such as conditions that require them to be on oxygen, to have a feeding tube, to have special treatment for diabetes, and so on. They will have their needs taken care of on a twenty-four-seven basis. This will include housekeeping, laundry services, toileting,

activities of daily living, meals, and medication. Like assisted-living facilities, residential care homes might come with transportation services,
and they often set up activities for residents. Residents may also receive
opportunities to take up hobbies, go on outings, and learn more about
the others around them during their stay. Some homes might offer specialized care, such as help for Alzheimer's patients or dementia-related
services.

This type of setting is small and personal. A residential care home,
depending on the state's regulation, might have between six and ten
seniors living in it. Individuals who want a home setting and customized care (and who doesn't?!) will find that appealing. This living option is typically more affordable than nursing homes in the same area.
Residents may pay between $3,000 and $12,000 a month. The exact
cost will depend on the assessment of the individual's medical needs and
care plan as well as other factors, such as where the home is located.

People who live in a residential care home usually say that they find
it quieter than an assisted-living facility or nursing home. These places
are typically located in neighborhoods full of traditional houses and
generally have a staff-to-patient ratio between one to three and one to
six, depending on the home. Caregivers in the home must meet certain
requirements, such as having nursing-assistant or healthcare-aide certification. Each state has its own set of standards that residential care home
owners and workers must meet in order to operate and remain open.

WHAT IT COULD MEAN TO MOVE TO A FACILITY

Now that we've had an overview of the options available for seniors
when they need more care, let's look at what it's really like when they
have to move out of their home and into a different place. I'll give you
an example to set the scene. Let's say I'm in my office, going over some

paperwork for my residential care home business. My phone rings, and it's an unknown number. "Hello, this is Nelly," I say.

"Hi, Nelly, I got your number from Ann[15]—she is the daughter of Cathy, one of your residents," says the voice on the other end of the line in a rush.

"Oh, she is a lovely person," I say. I sense the anxiety coming over the line and want to soothe the atmosphere. "Tell me, what's your name and how can I help?"

"My name is John, and I'm sorry to sound so crazed, but the truth is, I am at my wit's end. You see, I've been trying to help my wife take care of her mother, and my mother-in-law is really a wonderful person. Or was. I mean, we love her very much. But she just needs a lot more care now than she has needed in the past. It is getting really hard to help, and we're starting to worry about her. A lot."

"I see," I say slowly, to help maintain a sense of calm. "Trust me when I say you are not the first person to call me and say something like this. It is a very common thing. Now, let me try to get a better picture of what's going on, because I want to help you. Is she living with you and your wife?"

"No, she's in her own home, and that's the problem. My wife and I can't take her into our own house; we don't have room. But we are trying to care for her by going over to her place and helping. First it was once a week, then once a day, and now my wife has had to cut back on her hours at work. We're really strapped, and to be honest, I'm feeling like we are all going crazy. My mother-in-law isn't happy, my wife is worried about her safety since it is really hard for her mom to get around the house on her own, and I'm afraid a disaster is about to strike. We can't go on like this."

Can you sense the tension in this scene? I think it's pretty easy to see that this son-in-law and his wife have been trying their best to help.

They are feeling really stressed. They know they have to do something like moving her to a setting where she can get more care. That's hard for them to think about, just as it is equally hard for them to try to take care of her on their own, knowing that it isn't enough.

But now let's take it to another level. Think about that mother. How do you think she feels? She's been living in her own home and managing by herself, maybe for years. Now she has needed more help recently and either knows or senses that she is going to have to leave. She will have to go to a new place she's not familiar with and be surrounded by new people and schedules. Talk about trauma.

And *traumatic* is the word I often use to describe these changes. Anyone who has to leave their own home faces a major psychological transition. This is a big challenge. In fact, it is so hard for seniors to move out of a home where they may have lived for forty, fifty, or even sixty years that they usually won't do it on their own. They will sometimes have to be forced, in a way, out of their primary residence. By that I mean they will almost always wait until they have no other option. For instance, they might fall and fracture their hip, leg, or ankle. Suddenly they can't live at home on their own anymore because they can't get around self-sufficiently. They need surgery or therapy, or both, before they can even begin to think of recovering. Or they might have a stroke and be rushed to the emergency room, and after the stroke incident, the family decides that Mom or Dad cannot live on their own anymore. They simply aren't strong enough or healthy enough to do it.

Very few people will go to a facility that offers more assistance before they reach that point in time when they really need a higher level of care. As we have seen, most seniors would prefer to retire and stay at home for the rest of their lives. When they realize they can't remain in their own home and have no other choice but to move to a care facility, it really has an emotional effect on them.

And how does this psychological impact play out? Let me tell you, I

could see it in action on the faces of seniors when I worked in larger facilities. These older folks would carry looks of great concern when they
were transferred from their home to a place they viewed as an institution.

For example, when I was working at an assisted-living facility and
a new resident would arrive, I would greet them and try to get to know
them a little bit. One of the first things they would ask me would be
"Does this mean I am never going back to my home? Will I be dying
soon?"

You could see by how they acted that they thought there was no
hope of going back to their homes. Most of the time, their family would
sign a contract for long-term care. This would mean, to the seniors, that
they were going to be in the facility for an extended period—probably
for the remainder of their lifetimes. They would sit in a new chair, or
in their old chair that had now been abruptly placed in a new setting,
and look around. They would be thinking, "I won't see my house again.
I won't see my yard again. I'll never visit with my neighbors next door
again." And they would certainly be worried about losing their independence. Take a moment and imagine what else must be going on in
their heads during that moving time. Talk about a drastic psychological
change.

Bear in mind that when these transitions are taking place, it's not
uncommon for the senior to have dementia or Alzheimer's. I've witnessed what happens when elderly folks with early-stage memory loss
have to leave their homes, and it can make them very agitated because it
is so hard for them to understand the reasons for the move. I've also seen
individuals in advanced stages of memory loss feel extremely stressed
during this transition. All of a sudden they see a myriad of new faces and
activities, which only increases their levels of confusion.

In most cases, the senior's family—rather than the senior—makes
the decisions surrounding the transition. This can cause further frustration for the older individual. Talk about feeling like things are spinning

out of control: the senior no longer calls the shots, let alone cares for themselves.

Now, think about what that senior who moves into a large facility might be facing in the months ahead. Perhaps the staff serves breakfast every day at 7:00 a.m. A tray of fruit and yogurt is placed in front of the older person. And as they look at it, they remember how they used to enjoy sleeping in until 7:30 or 8:00 a.m. every morning, having a coffee with cream and sugar at about 9:00 a.m., and making themselves some eggs and toast after that. While they are picturing this and daydreaming a little bit, the caregiver enters their room and says, "Breakfast time is over." The tray is taken away before they even realize it's there. (This may not happen at every facility! But I am giving an example to show that it is hard to offer personalized care and be sufficiently sensitive to changes in a senior's level of independence.)

This is just one of the countless examples of how seniors are suddenly much more dependent on others for everything that happens, and when it happens, during the course of their days. Many will feel like they are a burden (which, by the way, seniors never want to be—and feeling like this can even be risky to their health). Ultimately, as they adjust to being in a facility, residents may get the sense that they are just on a big conveyor-belt setup, so to speak, of served meals, doled-out medications, and bedding changes.

For many reasons, seniors sometimes view going to a large facility as a last resort. It's not unusual to hear older people, after moving to an assisted-living center or nursing home, ask their family members not to come and visit them. That sounds strange, doesn't it? But based on what we've already explored in the previous chapter, it's a little more understandable. These seniors don't want to rely on others to take care of them. They feel sad and like they've lost their sense of privacy and the little things in life that were important to them. They might not like the food and just feel down about life overall. They don't want anyone to see them in this sad mood, unable to care for themselves. It's a little embarrassing and more than a little stressful.[16]

LONG-TERM WELL-BEING ISN'T EASY

Looking past this initial phase of moving in to a large facility, studies have shown that while some seniors might adapt to life in a nursing home or assisted-living center after several months, others might sink further into a state of depression. This is especially likely if the elderly residents aren't taken outside regularly to get a healthy dose of sunshine and vitamin D. It can also occur if patients are capable of doing some physical activity but don't have the chance to exercise often. Another reason for this downturn stems from the lack of social interaction, as seniors are often intensely lonely and may feel isolated. Even the quality of food can have an impact: if it is not nutritious, it might negatively affect seniors' well-being. In all, as they settle in, about 20 percent of all nursing-home residents have major depression, and another 30 percent present significant depressive symptoms.[17]

Fixing this depression problem isn't as easy as offering some antidepressant pills. We need to be really careful when giving older people medicine, and just pumping more chemicals into their system is not always the answer. Doctors have reported that sometimes they give older people medication for depression and those folks show zero sign of improvement. Others might feel happier but then have to deal with the side effects and other problems that stem from the antidepressants mixing with other medications they are taking. They might have a greater chance of falling, for instance. That is a serious risk for an older person who may already have some mobility issues.[18]

I'm not the only one to have noticed this effect while working with the elderly. One psychiatrist in particular, Dr. Jules Rosen, spent years prescribing antidepressant medications to his older patients in nursing homes and assisted-living facilities and observed little improvement among them. Frustrated by this, he decided to explore what was going on via an experiment. He wanted to see if therapies and activities, rather than more pills, could help improve the mood of older people living in facilities. He rationalized that recreation is essential for all people, regardless of their age. An eighty-year-old man, for instance, might feel relaxed by taking a leisurely Sunday drive, reading in his favorite chair, or watching his favorite program on television. But these refreshing pastimes become problematic in a nursing home. Suddenly the man can't get up and go on a Sunday drive. His family members sold his favorite chair on eBay. And while he can go play bingo every Monday night, he'd rather be watching his show, which he can't find on the cable hookup at the nursing home.[19] Even if the show is available through the cable connection, his roommate might not like the show, and so he has to switch channels to find a program they both agree on. As Dr. Rosen observed, it's no wonder the elderly will frequently feel depressed upon entering an institution and may struggle with depression simply due to the fact that they must make a new life for themselves at an old age and in such a different environment.

Dr. Rosen, along with his colleagues, got to work developing a program to lift the spirits of depressed nursing-home residents as an alternative to medication. Together they created a plan to study what would happen if older folks were given opportunities to engage in recreational activities that were similar to ones they had enjoyed before entering a long-term-care facility. Dr. Rosen and his coworkers identified thirty-two elderly residents of a Pennsylvania nursing home who had depression. More than half these individuals had mild to moderate dementia, but all were able to participate in some form of recreation.

An interesting thing to note about this study is that about 50 percent of the residents who participated in it had been on medication for depression for a month before they started the new program. When the study began, these residents hadn't shown any signs of improvement in their mood, even after thirty days of pills. During the study, the medical team didn't make any adjustments to their medications—the only things they changed were their activities.

So what happened? First, the residents in the study met with a therapist who helped them set up a program that included activities they used to do in and outside their own homes. Then they set up a schedule that included some of these new fun things. The plan was to do these activities for six weeks in a row.

The fun was about to begin. Four residents who loved to play cards decided to meet twice a week. At their meetings, they would pull out their decks and play to their hearts' content. A gentleman in the study said he used to love playing golf, back before he had a stroke. So the doctors got him a putting iron and miniature putting green. Once a week in the nursing home, he set up the putting green in a long hallway and got to play, putting away. He was having such a good time that other residents paid attention. Several elderly women started watching his golf outings and then made bets on whether he could make a putt.

Another resident in the study said he loved to watch the Pittsburgh Steelers play football but had stopped tuning in after moving into the nursing home. The reason? He didn't like watching the game alone. It was too sad and lonely for him to watch TV by himself. For the study, the workers reserved a television lounge in the nursing home where the man and his family and friends could gather on Sunday afternoons and watch the Steelers.

After six weeks, the medical team gathered to analyze the results. They noted that more than half the residents who had participated showed no more signs of depression. Others had seen some improvement in their mood. Moreover, the residents who recovered from their depression said that after the six weeks of scheduled activities, their social needs had been met.

This might seem like a happy story, but unfortunately, here is where it takes a downturn. The study finished after six weeks, as planned, and afterward, the nursing home stopped providing the activities that had been set up. All the residents who had recovered from their depression lapsed right back into it. The study concluded that while social engagements and activities really helped nursing-home residents, the setup just wasn't sustainable. The nursing home wasn't able to make individual recreational programs available to its seniors.[20]

This is so sad, but it can and sometimes does happen in nursing homes across the country. By and large, they just aren't set up to build the ongoing active schedule that can be so rewarding and healthy for seniors. As a result, older folks can get depressed, which can even shorten their life expectancy.

Even if they do find a way to manage, it's important to note that the trauma sustained during the transition phase isn't necessarily relieved. Think about this scenario: Say you move into a large facility and adjust, as best you can, to the new lifestyle, along with its ups and downs. You don't really like it, but you've decided to make do. Then one day you feel sick, and during the coming months you get sicker. Finally, one day you are so ill that the facility decides they can't help you anymore. They call 911. Suddenly you're put on a gurney and shoved into an ambulance. It takes you to a hospital, where you are surrounded by people you don't know. Would you be feeling more cared for or more traumatized at that moment?

For many, this situation is simply inevitable. It is a possible path in a senior's life.

MOVING INTO A RESIDENTIAL CARE HOME

From a psychological standpoint, for a senior there is a big difference between moving to a smaller setting and moving to a large facility, after leaving their home. Let's look at my residential care homes to see how seniors cope with the transition to a more personalized space. To start with, the moment a senior enters, they are usually reminded of their own home. That's because the environment they see is a small setting, in a house, complete with bedrooms, a living room, a kitchen, and a view. And you know what? Sometimes that view from the window of this new residential care home is even better than what they had in their previous home. They might be looking at a beautiful, well-cared-for flower patch and not the rocky path or overgrown garden they had at their old place.

Entering a smaller home and meeting just five new people is a 180-degree difference compared to entering a nursing home filled with a hundred or more beds. The same is true for the caregiver transition. A new resident at my residential care homes meets just a handful of people, who will quickly become familiar faces as they help and care for them. If that same person went into a nursing home, seeing all those staff workers racing around could be pretty overwhelming.

This sense of familiarity, from seeing a place that looks like a home to meeting a smaller group of people, can really help ease the strain of moving. Certainly, all residents who enter one of my residential care homes will go through a transition period. They will be facing, on a psychological level, the fact that they had to leave their home. But by and large, moving to a residential care home is a much less traumatic experience for a senior. It usually takes less time to adjust and feel comfortable in their new surroundings.

And rather than feeling let down and like they ought to give up, residents might find hope and motivation once they move in. This was the case for an elderly couple who were both in their eighties when they became residents in one of my residential care homes. As I was getting to know them, one of the first things they asked me was "Will we be able to go back home?" Sounds familiar, doesn't it? Indeed, I had been asked this exact question, as we saw earlier, time after time when working in large facilities.

But this time, in my residential care home, I could give a personalized answer. I looked at their situation and saw that the couple was inn good overall health. In their case, the wife had fractured her hip and was having a hard time getting around. That was the main reason they had come to me. I knew my staff could work with them and make sure the wife got all the therapy she needed to recover. I shared this with the couple.

You know what? My staff did get started with the couple right away. We made sure they were eating a healthy diet, with plenty of water and vegetables, and that the wife had all the chances in the world to do the exercises she was supposed to do while her hip healed. A year and a half later, she was moving around again. The couple left the residential care home and returned, happily, to their own home.

Can you imagine how their lives might have gone if they had instead chosen to go with a larger care facility? What if they had been sent to a nursing home and the wife didn't like it? What if she wasn't motivated to do the physical therapy she needed to do to get better? Maybe the wife wouldn't have cared for the food served and, as a result, wouldn't have absorbed the nourishment that was an essential part of her recovery process. They might not have been surrounded by a caring, doting staff who were ready to talk to them about the challenges they were facing and give them hope by reminding them of all the fun things they could do again after the recovery period. Their story really could have ended differently. They might have faced more traumatic times or, worse, never returned to the home they longed for.

Now, I should point out here that we can't, and don't, promise every single resident who comes into my residential care homes that they will be able to return to their own home someday. At the end of the day, some residents have specific conditions that might not make returning to their own homes a viable option. And technically, any resident can decide for themselves if they want to leave; they're not legally bound to stay in my residential care homes. From a practical perspective, however, in the case of this couple, I could see that their health history indicated they did have a good chance of making a full recovery. I also knew that they were motivated to return home and that my staff was capable of providing the help they needed during their rehab journey. In sum, we were able to take the time to look at a specific situation and offer recommendations based on the couple's exact circumstances.

Elderly folks who stay longer than a year and a half in a residential care home often find their new life to be an agreeable one. And more than that: they may be surrounded with happier, sunnier options than are available at a larger facility. My residents are much more likely to avoid falling into a depression. They are surrounded by caregivers who treat them with love and respect and are eager to do little things to accommodate their personalities and preferences.

The study Dr. Rosen carried out showed how happy people are when they can do what they used to do or at least get a taste of their previous lifestyle; my residential care homes make that part of our everyday practice. I didn't need a study to realize this; I set the system up based on my own intuition and what I knew about elderly people, including my grandmom. I never wanted anyone to feel like they were walking into an institution or a place where they would face a long, slow decline.

Instead, when a new resident moves in, we ask, "What did you like to do when you were at home?" Maybe someone responds that they loved to get up late and have coffee at 10:00 a.m. That's great, and we can make that happen every day for that person. Maybe they enjoyed reading in a chair and napping in the afternoon. We could get them set up for that and find books that they will love. More importantly, these little things can be done on a consistent basis. There's no need to stop after six weeks like Dr. Rosen and his colleagues did. And those ongoing measures really do help keep smiles on the residents' faces.

They also tend to keep family members smiling. It's usually obvious to them that their loved one is getting lots of social interaction and being well cared for. Trust me, when an adult child visits a parent who is struggling in a large facility like a nursing home, they can see signs that their parent is really down. The older person might rarely—or never—smile, or just seem unmotivated. That's a big difference from the sunny faces and good cheer that are prevalent in my homes.

This environment is exactly what I yearned for when I was working at nursing homes and other large care facilities. I longed to sit down with residents and really get to know them as people. I wanted to treat each one like I had cared for my own grandmom. I knew she would want the type of home-care setting I could provide. What's more, she would have wanted to keep doing her favorite things as much as possible. She would have wanted to eat good, homemade food, just like our residential care homes provide.

Under my residential care home model, the trauma of moving to a new home tends to quickly subside for new residents. And that stress can stay at bay, even when tough times happen. If an older person needs to go to the emergency room, a caregiver always accompanies them. This is very different from the scenes I saw in some large facilities, where the staff might call for help, wheel the person out, and wish them the best of luck in the future. My model, on the other hand, requires an attendant to go along so the resident feels safe and knows that they have an advocate right at their side. This is especially important when that person has dementia or Alzheimer's and is unable to advocate for themselves. We send someone who knows what that person has been experiencing and can communicate this to the medical team at the hospital. All these measures have the potential to reduce the stress of the situation and help the senior feel more at ease and, more importantly, get the right treatment.

STAYING SAFE

When illnesses break out, one problem that nursing homes often face is a result of the sheer number of residents and how closely they live together. One person gets a cough, and pretty soon hacking can be heard from every room down the hall. Residents everywhere are asking for cough drops to soothe their dry and sore throats. The CDC reports that up to 380,000 residents in long-term-care facilities die each year from infections.[21]

This is one of the reasons why, when the flu season arrives in fall, it's common practice for nursing homes and other large care institutions to make sure their residents get the flu vaccine. They want to keep everyone as healthy as possible.

But what happens when a new illness enters the scene? That's exactly what we saw in 2020, when COVID-19 swept through the headlines and nursing homes across America. Suddenly, the elderly were at risk in a big way. Nursing-home caregivers and their residents were scared, and rightly so.

The outbreak quickly infiltrated care facilities and put the elderly, the most vulnerable group in terms of age and health conditions, at risk. In May 2020, the *New York Times* reported that one-third of all US coronavirus deaths were nursing-home residents or workers. At that time, the virus had infected more than 7,700 facilities. The article also stated that the virus was spreading more easily through spaces where many people lived in a confined environment and workers moved from room to room.[22]

It is natural to assume many families were very worried about their loved ones in long-term-care facilities. In fact, they had reason to be anxious about more than just their aging relative's chances of getting sick. The virus also led to skyrocketing levels of loneliness. In Colorado, for instance, most residents in nursing homes did not see anyone from the outside world between March and June, due to a state public-health order designed to protect residents from the spread of the virus. "Loneliness . . . is linked to poor health indicators," said Dr. Sheri Gibson, a gero-psychologist at the University of Colorado Colorado Springs. "Among older adults, it has even been linked to early mortality."[23]

The isolation and lack of a sense of security quickly took their toll. "For the length that it has gone on, it is just wearing away at the people here," said Claudia, a resident at a nursing home in Colorado. "The people that were ill before are getting more ill, [and] the people that were depressed, they're getting more depressed."[24]

Other places around the country felt a similar effect. In Iowa, at the beginning of the outbreak, nearly 50 percent of COVID deaths took place in care facilities. In Texas, almost 80 percent of the residents in one nursing home in San Antonio were infected. The National Guard had to evacuate a nursing home outside Nashville, Tennessee, after about a hundred people contracted the virus and four of them died. The risk of getting the disease, in fact, was so great that in California, the public-health director for Los Angeles advised families to take their loved ones out of nursing homes.[25]

In my own state, Washington, we had similar situations in large care institutions. In June 2020, the Adult Family Home Council reported that 60 percent of skilled-nursing facilities and 35 percent of assisted-living facilities within the state had had some type of COVID outbreak. Small group homes, however, were not affected nearly as much. By that time, just 5 percent of residential care homes across the state had dealt with an outbreak.[26]

At a personal level, I went to extra lengths to ensure my residential care homes had all the measures they needed to be safe places for the elderly. I'm proactive by nature, and when I first saw bits of news fore-shadowing the outbreak, I stocked up on essentials like sanitizer. Weeks later, when everyone frantically raced to buy cleaning supplies, I sat back and surveyed the well-stocked shelves in my residential care homes. We were ready.

The daughter—we'll call her Mary[27]—of one of my residents decided to put this to the test. She explained to me that she was a doctor and understood the precautions she needed to take. But then she begged to come in and see and hold her mom. I said, "Mary, I respect the fact that you want to see your mom, but at the same time, you realize I am here to take care of your mom. I have a duty to protect your mother and the other residents who are under my care during this epidemic."

"But I'm a doctor," she insisted.

"Coronavirus doesn't care if the daughter is a doctor or not," I replied.

She kept asking for permission to come inside and embrace her mom. In fact, she had some decent reasons for wanting to see her. Not that her mom was sick; quite the contrary. Her mom hadn't been walking in February of that year, but then, after some months in my home with my caregivers, she had started walking again.

"I'm so happy she is walking and I want to hug her," Mary explained on one phone call.

"I'm happy for both of you too," I said. "But if you really love her, you should remember that love and wait. When coronavirus has moved on, I want you to hug your mom and take her out so you can have a nice lunch with her. But if you get in close contact with her now, she might get sick and you might not have that chance later."

I urged her to not visit inside, per the government COVID-related guidelines, for the safety of her mother and the other residents. Our conversation repeated itself numerous times. Mary was pretty frustrated, but she recognized my concern for her family.

Several weeks later, she sent me a text with a different tone. "You're an angel," she said. She was referring to our conversations regarding coronavirus and the visiting rules. She went on to explain that she respected me for putting my foot down. "The way you protected my mom," she said, "it's like she's part of the family."

I was able to have this type of personal communication during COVID with residents and family members because of our small numbers. We are not a large facility, where family members frequently are asked to go through vast amounts of paperwork to find answers to their questions. Instead, I could look them right in the eye and explain the measures we were taking for their loved ones.

This close communication had an additional benefit related to safety. As soon as the pandemic hit, we explained to families that every time their loved one was exposed to an outside source, there was a chance that they would get infected with COVID. Given this, we evaluated what was essential for their aging relative and what could wait. For instance, routine appointments and physical therapy sessions could often be postponed. We also suspended all nonessential services, such as manicures and pedicures. Instead of bringing people in from the outside to give nail treatments, our staff trimmed nails for our residents during the pandemic.

In addition to looking out for the residents, we took precautions for the caregivers in our homes. When news of COVID hit the headlines, I offered staff the opportunity to sleep in vacant guesthouse attachments on our properties so they wouldn't have to worry about going home and getting or bringing infections. If they wanted to stay on-site, they had that option. Also, some of our caregivers worked in several different caregiving environments. I made an agreement with them that I would provide all the hours they needed to support themselves if, in exchange, they would avoid going to other care facilities. This had a twofold benefit: it reduced the risk of infection and also gave caregivers the peace of mind that they wouldn't lose their jobs.

This was not the case in other care institutions across the country.

Even before COVID, many nursing homes and assisted-living centers were having a hard time keeping their workers. Charlene Harrington, an emeritus professor of nursing and sociology at the University of California, San Francisco, told *Stateline* in May 2020, "Seventy-five percent of all nursing homes did not meet the professional staffing standards that experts believed they should have before the virus hit. So that made them very vulnerable."[28]

When the disease broke out, many workers either called in sick because they had the virus or were too afraid to come to work, as they held the fear that they might get infected and pass the disease on to their families. This trend led to stretched-thin resources at the facilities. Caregivers sometimes had to care for even more patients than usual. As a result, the care provided was at risk of being poor or unacceptable for seniors. "When you're working short, you make decisions you may not make on a good day," Mairead Painter, a long-term advocate in Connecticut, told the same publication.[29]

Staff members at large care facilities who weren't paid well were sometimes quick to look for other jobs at gas stations or retail stores, where they might have thought there would be less chance of them getting sick. The average nurse aide makes about thirteen dollars an hour in a nursing home or assisted-living center.[30] And while some places offered workers bonuses for staying or gave them free meals, many care facilities simply couldn't afford to compensate their staff more.[31]

In contrast, my residential care homes had staff members who stayed on all the way through the course of the pandemic. These caregivers also had lower levels of stress, as we looked after their personal safety and financial well-being. Many of my staff members were personally attached to the residents, and they wanted to take good care of them at all times.

At my homes, residents didn't face the intense risk of isolation and loneliness. We still had caregivers around to chat with the seniors, ask them about their health, and do as much as possible to make their days seem normal. We could explain what was going on to residents and families and share our motivation to do what we could to protect them during the outbreak.

Still, it's important to note that even with all the safety measures in place, my residential care homes weren't completely immune. During the pandemic, one location did have some cases of COVID. Since we had a smaller number of seniors inside this home, and more caregivers tending to each one, we were able to manage better than other large institutions where each staff member oversaw a greater number of residents.

It's likely that the pandemic gave families throughout America the chance to evaluate the conditions of the place where their loved one was being cared for. Step back and consider what you would want for your own aging relative. Would you feel comfortable moving them to a packed facility where you knew diseases could spread quickly? Or would it ease your worries to place them in a small, homelike setting, knowing that their chances of getting sick there were much lower? I think the virus has shown us that there are certain advantages to small group-home settings for the elderly.

And based on the other advantages we've seen for the residential care home environment, it's easy to see why a family might choose it over a large care institution. If an older person has to leave their home, it makes sense to go to a place where they will feel loved and well cared for. A friendly place. One that feels like home. And that's just what my residential care home provides.

As you're likely guessing, there's more to my story (!), and I want to share it with you. In this chapter, we compared my model to others. To see the whole picture of my residential care design, we need to look at the other aspects, which include the financial side. Let's see how caring for seniors well and treating them as family can pay off in many ways (take notes, investors, providers, and caregivers!). That's exactly what we'll do in the next chapter.

CHAPTER 3

What Makes Residential Care Homes Unique

While we saw in the previous chapter that being involved in a residential care home business includes pouring love into seniors and their everyday lives, we also know that we need to be practical about our time and resources. We must consider the financial aspects when making choices. That's what we'll do in this chapter, as we look at the residential care business from an investment perspective. (In later chapters, we'll explore angles related to caregivers and providers.)

Here's what I found as I developed my own system in this industry: if they are set up the right way, residential care homes have the potential to generate significant income and cash flow. In fact, in some cases they can provide a stronger return than other types of real estate investing.

But don't just take my word for it. Let's get a full picture of how a residential care home investment is truly unique and can be beneficial for your portfolio. First, we'll look at the fact that there is a growing demand to house the aging population in the United States. We'll also sift through the history of care facilities from a real estate perspective to see why some are crumbling and others are rising. Finally, we'll take a look at investing in different types of real estate and at the specific benefits residential care homes can bring.

SENIOR CARE IN HIGH DEMAND

Thanks to advances in medicine, people are expected to live longer than they did several decades ago. The average person in the United States lived for just sixty-six years in 1955.[32] Compare that to today, when the average American lives to be seventy-eight years old.[33] From a physical point of view, the older people get, the more likely it is that they will need help going about their days. By 2031, some of the first baby boomers will turn eighty-five years old.[34] That same year, experts are predicting that more than three million people will have dementia and need to receive care for it.[35] It is estimated that by 2050, about fifteen million seniors in the United States will need long-term care.[36]

This growing segment of elderly individuals brings a change to the real estate scene. Rather than living in their independent homes, seniors are looking for places that will provide more care at a certain point. This means that the need for properties with greater levels of assistance is high—and will be increasing. And as we'll see, seniors' tastes in properties where they can receive care have changed over the years.

HISTORY OF CARE FACILITIES

In the United States, caring for the elderly on a large scale originated with nursing homes. These were followed by assisted-living facilities and then by care options like home help and residential care homes. Let's start at the very beginning, back when the country was recovering from the Great Depression.

The first time we really saw nursing homes pop up was in the 1930s.

In 1935, the federal government passed the Social Security Act, which sought to help older people in general. The government also created a program for seniors called the Old Age Assistance.[37] These initiatives helped fund nursing homes, and by the time the United States entered the 1960s, over nine thousand nursing homes had been built. These homes were, by and large, backed by federal money. By 1965, more than three hundred thousand seniors throughout the country lived in nursing homes.[38]

While these historical facts might seem like a good setup at first glance, the reality is that many of these places were not fully regulated. This led to a slew of problems, including elder abuse, less than ideal care, and poor living conditions.[39] Unfortunately, many seniors weren't happy in these large institutions that had been built especially for them.

During the following years, nursing homes faced more problems. Some managers struggled to pay for maintenance and to keep their places running efficiently. Others didn't get what they considered to be enough federal funding to cover their costs. These financial challenges and run-down facilities caused a drop in residents. After a time, some nursing homes even had to close their doors because they just couldn't keep up.

Still, when families chose not to send their loved ones to a nursing home, they knew their aging relatives needed someplace to stay. In response to this demand, assisted-living facilities entered the scene in the 1960s. They were designed to offer retirees more benefits, like cooked meals and activities with other seniors in the same place. At first, assisted-living facilities didn't usually include medical services. Instead, residents could have a doctor or medical professional come see them at the facility and care for them there.

In general, seniors and their families tended to like the assisted-living option better than nursing homes. In response to this trend, companies built more of these centers. By 2016, there were 28,900 assisted-living facilities in the United States.[40] That figure was higher than the number of nursing homes, which stood at 15,600 during the same year.[41]

By then, however, there were more options available, including a long list of healthcare-service companies. These firms would bring care and treatment to seniors in their own homes. This meant that older folks could get assistance with their daily activities. They might have someone come and deliver meals, help them carry out therapeutic exercises, monitor medical conditions, and take medications.

These healthcare-service companies became known as home-health providers. In 2016, there were more than 12,200 home-health-provider groups.[42] This trend coincides with what we learned in the previous chapter where we talked about how many seniors prefer to stay at home and age in place. With this type of setup, they can remain in their houses for, really, as long as possible.

While this may initially sound like a good deal—a home-health provider that enables a senior to age in place—families often discover major drawbacks. It can be tough for an adult child to manage this type of care, for one. Say the adult child lines up care and someone is scheduled to come and help their parent every Monday. What if that person calls in sick? Suddenly that adult child is stuck with no one to come and assist their parent.

In addition, home healthcare doesn't usually provide twenty-four-seven care (and if this is an option, you'll have to explore costs, as it tends to be priced high compared to other eldercare services available). Treatment for complicated conditions is generally unavailable. I could go on, but my point is that this home-healthcare concept ultimately does not solve the problems seniors face. Older people want to stay at home, but just having someone come in and help out a little is typically very hard on the family and is usually only a temporary solution. Eventually, the parent will often need more care and will have to move to a different place to get it.

That said, other initiatives to help out seniors at home have been implemented, and it's worth pointing out some of them. For example, at the state level, several changes have been made in recent years to accommodate the growing senior population. Almost all fifty states in 2019 and 2020 planned to offer different forms of support to the seniors in their communities.[43] Local programs designed networks to provide transportation for seniors, and cities created housing programs to give them low-cost places to live. For instance, elderly individuals might get a discount on bus services or a free meal at a nearby community center. Some cities also offer adult day-care services, where seniors can be brought to spend the day.

Today, nursing homes and assisted-living centers face significant challenges on several levels. Some facilities encounter issues related to high turnover rates and financial strain. Couple that with more ways for seniors to stay at home, and it's easy to see why some nursing homes and assisted-living centers have responded to these trends by closing their doors.

During this same time frame, as nursing homes and assisted-living centers struggled, smaller group homes for seniors entered the scene. They have, in many areas, sprung up as a grassroots movement.[44] Since they usually consist of residential homes, these smaller settings for seniors are sometimes easier to establish than a large care institution. As we learned in the previous chapter, residential care homes often provide seniors with more opportunities and more personalized treatment than other forms of care. This fact has led more seniors and their families to consider a residential care home as a housing option in recent years.[45]

INVESTING IN REAL ESTATE

Now that we've looked at the ebb and flow of senior housing options over the years, let's pivot and consider what it's actually like to invest in real estate. To start with, there's no clear one-size-fits-all path for making money in properties. Certain properties will bring specific opportunities, along with unique drawbacks. That's why it's important to consider what you would be getting into before you pursue any transactions or put down any cash.

That said, the market holds substantial opportunity. And more people are catching on to this: investing in real estate is an area that has gained popularity in recent years. At the end of 2018, investors made up 11.3 percent of all home sales in the US housing market, which reflected a twenty-year high since 1999.[46] Certainly there are investors who look to get involved in the industry on a large scale, but there are also other smaller investors in the space. They may buy a few homes over the years and then rent them out for decades to follow. This segment of smaller investors has grown as well.

For investors of all sizes who want to purchase property and rent it out, there are plenty of opportunities. The field where they can play is pretty big: in the United States, forty-four million households rented properties during 2022.[47] That's a lot of families looking to rent a place from an owner.

Traditionally, real estate investments have tended to be long-term. By that, we mean investors are usually looking at owning the place they buy for at least several years. Investors should also be aware that it isn't always as easy to move away from real estate as it is to release other investments. You can often sell a stock quickly, for instance. But with property, the investment isn't as liquid. Given this, investors usually adopt a committed, long-term mindset when purchasing real estate.

In its basic form, we might think of investing in real estate as purchasing a property—either through a loan or with funds you have on hand—and then bringing in rental income. In this setup, you are the landlord of a property. There are other ways to invest in real estate too. For instance, you might buy a place, fix it up, then sell it. Or you could join a real estate investment group or trust to bring in money. Finally, you might opt for senior-housing investments. In the following sections, we break each one down a bit more to help you get a clear concept of what we are talking about.

LANDLORD INVESTOR

With this option, you might oversee the purchasing of a property, or you could have a real estate agent help you find and buy it. You'll then have tenants who will pay you rent each month. You might manage these tenants or hire someone else to manage them. You'll also be responsible for repairs, and any contract work carried out at your property must meet the regulations and codes of your city.

If you want to go this route, you'll need a fair amount of capital to cover the initial costs and ongoing maintenance of a property. You'll also run the risk of not having tenants. For instance, if the property sits empty for a while, you'll still have to cover the expenses related to the investment.

One benefit of this setup is that rental properties can bring in regular income. You'll be able to write off many of the expenses as tax deductions. If you have losses, these can be balanced by any gains you might have received from other investments. If the property increases in value over time, when you sell it, you'll also likely make some profit on the sale.

Long-term rentals are what the National Real Estate Investors Association calls "the backbone of our nation's housing."[48] The association describes this type of rental as any residential property that has up to four units. While this doesn't usually include apartment buildings, it does account for single-family homes, duplexes, mobile homes, and quad units. You might decide to purchase and manage one of these types of housing units or even invest in several properties.

The downside to this option is that if you manage a place on your own, you can expect to spend many hours working on the details associated with it. You might get tenants who don't take good care of a yard or let the inside of the house deteriorate, for instance. They might leave the walls in dire need of a paint job, and you, as the owner, will need to provide a painter and a fresh bucket of paint.

It's also important to remember that home prices fluctuate. While they increased in value at a relatively steady rate from 1940 to 2006, they then dipped during the housing crisis from 2007 to 2009. In more recent history, the pandemic cast doubt on the housing market. Since then, investors have seen great resiliency in the residential care home industry, as it isn't as vulnerable to market fluctuations.[49]

OWNER-OCCUPIED RENTAL

If you have a place that you live in and also rent out, it's known as an owner-occupied rental. With this setup, you might have a duplex—you live in one unit and rent the other unit to a tenant. This can be handy, as you can build a network so that you know whom to call if there is a problem with the shower or if the garbage disposal breaks down. You'll also be pretty close to the other unit, so you can monitor what's going on.

A potential drawback to this arrangement is that, as we saw in the case of a landlord, you'll likely be responsible for all repairs and contractor work. You'll also probably have to spend a decent amount of time interacting with the other rental units. All this management can be draining and tiresome. For instance, you might be woken up in the middle of the night to check on a problem like a water leak.

In addition, all this closeness can take away from your privacy. Having a tenant as your next-door neighbor might mean you cross paths on a daily basis. If a tenant uses these meetups as a chance to continually point out what they'd like changed in their rental unit, you might soon be ready to move to a different place. And even if you have a solid relationship with the tenant, just the feeling of being watched can drive some owners to opt out of the housing deal.

VACATION RENTAL

If you're thinking of investing in real estate, you can't overlook the popularity of vacation rentals, coming to a place near you in the form of someone's house. Think Airbnb, Vrbo, Vacasa, and HomeToGo, to name just a few. In 2019, the overall revenue from vacation rentals came to nearly $58 billion.[50] By 2022, it was estimated to be above $80 billion.[51]

At first glance, this option just seems so easy. Practically all you have to do is step outside, post a few pictures of your home to a vacation-rental site or app, ask your renters to sign a few agreements, and watch the money flow in. If you have a second home or a vacation home in a popular spot, the process will seem like even more of a no-brainer. Let others stay in your place when you're not using it, right? Then pocket the dollars that come in from renters while you're away.

The downside of vacation rentals is actually the same downside we just discussed—it's so easy to do that almost everyone, it seems, is jumping on the bandwagon. In 2022, there were 1.5 million vacation rental listings in the United States.[52] If you live in a popular tourist destination, you might find that all your neighbors are also renting out their places, making it tough to get vacationers and revenue.

Another drawback is simply the risk of letting others into your property, as they might damage it or not maintain it properly. You'll also have to ensure that it meets industry standards. Visitors today expect, and even demand, a clean space. You'll need to provide enough bath towels, leave instructions for guests to show them how to turn on the TV, make sure the keys are passed on securely, and so on.

HOUSE FLIPPING

This type of investing is really a hands-on approach. If you have a background in real estate, construction, or renovating, this might have a big appeal. Flipping consists of first purchasing a property; often the place you'll buy is a residential home that needs serious work. You then invest the money needed to make repairs, do some renovations, and overall make the place shiny. Once it looks great, you put the "For Sale" sign back up and sell it for the best offer you can get. The amount you make depends on how much you paid to begin with, what you invested into the property, and, ultimately, the selling price. If all goes well, you can make a substantial return in a short time, in anywhere from several months to a year.

On the flip (!) side of flipping, there's a bit of luck involved with this process. Think about this worst-case scenario: you buy a house, fix it up, and make it look beautiful, and just when you are ready to sell it again, the market takes a dive. You could be out of the money you invested in fixing it up, and even some of what you paid for the house to begin with.

Other flippers might simply buy a house and then sell it. In these cases, they're hunting for places that have hidden value or properties in areas that are going up in price. If they see an undiscovered jewel, they jump on it. Then they wait a few months, up the price, and put the place back on the market. This is a bit like reselling or trading homes. It can work—and work well—but it is also laden with risk. Investors are just as likely to get burned as they are to win big.

Even with the potential negatives, this market has recently really grown in popularity. In 2018, people flipped almost 208,000 single-family homes and condos in the United States.[53] Part of this appeal may be that many people have seen the house-remodeling TV shows that are seemingly everywhere these days. These programs show how "easy" it can be to fix up a place: within a half hour—at least on TV—the place looks entirely different.

We should note, however, that it's often tricky to truly get a solid return on this type of investment. Consider this quick example: Say you buy a home, fix it up, and sell it for $60,000 more than you paid for it. Sounds pretty good, right? But what about the time, effort, and money you poured into fixing that place up? You might have had to pay for major and minor repairs, along with some remodeling projects. Utility bills, interest on a loan taken out for the home, and other necessary payments can quickly eat into your profit. And let's not forget those unfortunate surprises, like an issue with the foundation or a leaky roof that needs to be replaced. When the sale takes place, there are additional expenses to cover, including excise taxes and Realtor commissions. In sum, the process can be expensive, time-consuming, and less lucrative than you anticipated. Bringing in $60,000 after spending $75,000 on repairs doesn't sound like such a great deal anymore, does it?

RESIDENTIAL CARE HOMES

Now let's slow down the pace a little and really dive in to see what a good deal these can be. We'll start with how they are set up. Then, in the next section, we'll go over their unique advantages.

Residential care homes usually begin as homes in residential neighborhoods. An investor might purchase a home and then remodel it; these changes could include putting in a wheelchair ramp at the entrance, widening hallways and doorways to make them more accessible, and installing nonslip floors. The investor could then set up the residential care business on their own.

On the other hand, an investor could also work with a partner to buy the property or a ready-made residential care home and then establish their business. If you're an investor, you might receive income based on the number of residents in the home and what they pay. For landlords, the provider will pay rent, regardless of the number of residents living in the place.

WHY RESIDENTIAL CARE HOMES HAVE MORE OPPORTUNITIES

If you invest in a residential care home, you're getting into an arrangement with high potential. Let's begin with a cash-flow comparison. Say you purchase a three-thousand-square-foot home in a residential neighborhood. You rent it out to a nice family who pays you $3,500 each month. If you have a mortgage on the home for $2,500 every month, you'll subtract that from the $3,500 revenue. Your profit every month, then, will be $1,000.

Now take that exact same property and put a residential care home on it. There are two ways you can now get cash from this property. You can run the residential care business yourself, or you can rent it to someone else who will then run the business. Let's take some time to consider the potential profits on both these options.

If you run the residential care home yourself, you might have six residents who pay $8,000 each in rent every month. Your gross revenue would be $48,000. From that amount, you'll have to pay for your expenses, like the care team, food, and utilities. After paying for everything needed to run the business, your profit might be $25,000 a month.

Now let's review the other scenario for a moment. If you own the property and rent it to someone else who then runs the business, you can still bring in a steady profit. Using our same example from above, with six residents paying $8,000 each, you might expect to get between $8,000 and $10,000 a month. That's the rent that's getting sent your way from the person running the residential care home.

We'll explain exactly how those numbers would play out later on in the book. For now, it's sufficient to note that, either way, the cash flow is substantial. While running the business yourself may yield a higher profit, keep in mind that in either case, having a residential care home on that property is much more lucrative than renting it to a single family. We're talking about a difference that could potentially be in the tens of thousands of dollars per month.

These examples of the solid cash opportunities are really just the beginning. There are more ways that having a residential care home on a property can bring a higher return than other types of real estate investments. For instance, let's consider the case I mentioned in which you have a residential care home on a property and you lease it to someone who will run it. This person who will run the business is known as the provider. If you write up a lease with a provider, the terms of it will literally span years. Yes, you heard me correctly: years.

Generally speaking, the leases for residential care homes are always longer than leases on residential homes. For a residential home, you might expect to lease the property for a year. After twelve months, the family will often move out, and you will have to look for a new tenant. Or the home could sit vacant for several months or even longer. This vacancy could really reduce your cash flow. On the other hand, a residential care home is usually leased for between five and ten years. Long leases often mean less exposure and less risk. (When we think about it, we can see why landlords love having a long-term reliable tenant!)

Furthermore, it's worth pointing out that residential care homes tend to be noncyclical. This contrasts with the residential-rental industry. For instance, renters of residential homes might stay for six months or a year and then leave, due to a job change or desire to live in a different location with less expensive housing. For investors of residential care homes, the income takes a different pattern. If you run the business yourself, you'll likely be dealing with residents who remain long-term.

For arrangements with a provider, the lease might cover years. As such, the provider will pay month after month over the course of time. Given these differences, a residential care home investment might not face the same type of risk as other properties that could lose renters if economic conditions change.

Choosing a residential care home, then, brings you an opportunity to have a built-in cushion of security. You can often count on having a higher monthly income, a long-term lease, and noncyclical cash flows. Let's not forget, too, that more and more seniors are looking for this exact housing option.

I need to put a quick caveat in here to explain that not all residential care homes are the same. Essentially, a residential care home is a business built on a piece of real estate. This makes it different from some of the other real estate investments we listed. In flipping, for instance, you're just buying a place (hopefully at the right time!) and then selling it (again, hopefully when it's increased in value on the market and you can profit). With a residential care home, we're talking about an ongoing business in a residential home. It leans toward a commercial investment, even though the place appears to be a family home. This means that the way it's maintained and run will ultimately affect how much income can be generated from it. Having the right partner, with the know-how and expertise to set it up correctly, will increase your chances of getting the highest return possible on this type of investment.

We have seen how residential care home investments are really in a class of their own. In the next chapters, we'll look at them in detail. I'll show you everything that is involved in this type of an investment, and what approach you can take if you decide to do it on your own. I'll also lay out how this investment works if you use a partner for the process. (Quick pro tip: it's much easier with a partner! But we'll get to that later.) I'll list ways that caregivers and providers benefit in the arrangements that are made. Through it all, we'll see how being involved in the residential care business can be a way to create value for seniors, their loved ones, and your own personal well-being and wealth. With the right model, everyone can win, as we work together to create great living spaces and improve the quality of life for the aging population.

CHAPTER 4

Exploring Your
Investment Options

Let's imagine for a moment that we are getting together to have a coffee. You've come to me because you're interested in this residential care home investment idea and think it would be a great way to build wealth. You're also keen on the opportunity to help America's aging society and their families. Since I have experience in these areas, we've decided to spend a little time talking about how this all works.

That's how I want you to envision these next chapters: think of them as a back-and-forth, with you asking questions and expressing interest in learning more and me sharing with you some of the logistics regarding how this type of investment works. You can be confident that I won't sugarcoat anything: if something is tough, I'll say it straight up. That's the way I am. I don't like to beat around the bush or exaggerate: people need facts and appreciate clarity. In my world, this honest talk is something I guarantee.

With that in mind, let's get you ready for our coffee appointment by quickly recapping what we covered in the first chapters. This will give us a good baseline for what follows. You'll recall that we've seen there's a growing segment of older Americans who are currently, or will soon be, in need of more daily assistance. They can't care for themselves on their own anymore, and there's no one who can sufficiently oversee their daily needs at home. Many of these individuals have to move to a new place where they can get the care they need, but they want to avoid an institution-like residence. Instead, they prefer a homelike setting where they can get personalized attention. Their families want this too.

We also went over some of the main investment options in the real estate world. We observed the history of senior facilities and looked at recent market trends. Along the way, we compared some pros and cons of the latest choices for real estate investments. Through this study, we observed that being involved in the residential care home business offers an opportunity for providers and caregivers to generate an income and play a role in improving the quality of life for seniors. For investors, it can offer high cash flow, long-term leases, and an overall sense of security. This type of investment really outshines other real estate opportunities on today's market.

Now, let me offer you a seat and pour you some coffee. As you sip, I'm going to spend some time showing you how to tie those two concepts—an aging population and a growing real estate opportunity in residential care homes—together. Essentially, I'll walk you through how a residential care home investment can play out in real life. I'll show how investors can participate in this space (we'll briefly touch on providers and caregivers too—and go more in depth into both of these in a later chapter).

You'll notice this isn't something that can easily be done over the phone, because it's not a topic we can cover in a quick ten-minute chat. It's a bit more complicated than that. As with many types of investments, there are different approaches that can be taken to meet your goals.

In the following sections, we'll take a brief look at the two main ways a residential care home can be set up as an investment. The first of these is what I call the DIY, or do-it-yourself, approach. This method is based on the idea of building a residential care home business yourself and running it on your own. The second of these is known as the investor approach. It's designed to have you work with a partner. With this method, the partner will oversee the setting up and running of the home.

After introducing and defining these two approaches in this chapter, we'll use Chapters 5 and 6 to further dive into each one. Essentially, we'll lay out the details of both the DIY and the investor method. Regardless of how you decide to invest your funds, it's worth putting some thought into all the options that are available to you. Doing so will give you an inside look into the work that goes into these homes and how they operate on a day-to-day basis. Now, before your coffee cools, let's get started: we'll touch on the DIY approach first.

THE DO-IT-YOURSELF APPROACH

You know, I've noticed over the years that American culture tends to be enamored with the concept of DIY. Go to any Home Depot or home-improvement center and you'll see ads touting sales and discounts on the latest paints or tools. Walk through a Michaels store or any other arts-and-crafts center and you'll find aisles and aisles filled with little doodads you can use to make the most amazing artwork or hallway decoration, all from the comfort of your kitchen table. In addition to visiting these stores, you can view TV shows demonstrating how to declutter your house, watch YouTube channels outlining the latest DIY home repairs, and read magazines detailing how to build wooden furniture inside your own garage.

There's a reason for all this DIY fanfare: it can be appealing to make something on your own and take pride in your creation. Keep in mind, however, that all the examples we just laid out have one thing in common, and that is the fact that they are small-scale projects. Cleaning out a room, fixing the kitchen sink, assembling a chair . . . sure, they're all great. They also usually only require a few hours of your time and energy, and then you can call it a wrap.

I bring this up to stress the point that when I say DIY for a residential care home, I am not referring to these minor pursuits. I'm talking about a full-time, twenty-four-seven commitment. In other words, it is not your paint-by-number hallway picture. It is not your redone bedroom with a new color theme. It's far, far more time-consuming than a made-from-scratch Thanksgiving dinner.

Let me pause here and refill your coffee. Simply stated, a DIY real estate investment is a huge undertaking. If you decide to set up a residential care home on your own, you'll have to put in many hours of work before you can even start to think about opening the doors to welcome residents. You'll need certifications, licenses, employees, and on and on. And while you're setting it up, let's not forget this: you'll be shelling out or borrowing a ton of money at nearly every step. If you haven't done this before, there's a lot of risk involved. How do you know those dollars will bring that great return on investment we mentioned earlier?

Now, don't choke on your drink; I'm just telling you how it is, and I promised not to make anything rusty look shiny. It's important to see the reality of this DIY approach. When we discussed the perks of residential care home investments before, it was under the assumption that whoever is doing the heavy lifting (like setting up the property and starting the business) knows exactly what they are doing. For those who are well qualified, yes, there are wonderful benefits involved. For someone who is just starting out, the results might be similar to those small-scale projects we touched on: the first time you paint a bedroom, it probably won't look as nice as the fifth, sixth, or twentieth time you paint a room. It's just natural that projects get easier with experience. And that holds true for residential care home investments too. By the time you finish this chapter and the following two chapters, you'll see exactly what I mean.

For now, allow me to explain a bit more by outlining a few of the main challenges you'll find with the DIY system. This approach requires some unique skills and background that aren't generally necessary for common DIY home projects. You need a hefty amount of experience and expertise in both the real estate and senior-care industries, along with an ongoing passion for the tasks at hand. Oh, and one more thing: you'll have an advantage if you know how to start a business from the ground up. Specifically, I'm going to lay out four main areas: real estate knowledge, senior-care background, a passion for helping the elderly, and business know-how. Let's start with the real estate experience and expertise combo I mentioned.

If you want to create a residential care home on your own, you'll need to invest in property. You can do this either by buying the place with your own funds or taking out a mortgage for it. Every once in a while, I hear people make the statement that it would be easy to convert their own home into a residential care home business. Maybe so, maybe not. But whether you get a new place or convert a current one, you'll need to provide a dedicated space for your residents to live. And if you plan to live on the same property, you'll have to make some arrangements so the seniors can stay in one area while you and your family live in another. For example, maybe the residential care home space takes up the first floor of the home, and you live on the second floor. Even then, you'll have to decide if you want to be that close to the business. Typically, you'll also have to do some major remodeling, no matter what type of property you decide to use.

I mention this to show that knowing a thing or two about real estate is not just helpful; it's essential. Buy an overpriced piece of property and you're already increasing your risks by putting up too much unnecessary cash in the beginning. This could cause you to be financially strapped later in the process, as you'll need to bring in enough revenue to cover those initial expenses (which isn't easy to begin with, but we'll get to that later). If you don't have a strong real estate background, you might not know where to look for deals and how to accurately select the right home and best location for the business.

In addition to real estate expertise, you need a strong background in healthcare. This isn't just a good idea of mine: it's laid out by the law. The state in which you live will require a certain level of medical certification and experience in order to qualify for a license. And you'll need a license to be able to open your doors and receive residents. The amount of work you'll have to do will vary from state to state, but in general terms, we're talking about hundreds, or even more than a thousand, hours of experience in healthcare. There is generally a focus on senior-care experience as well. If you haven't spent all or part of your career in the medical field, you might have to dedicate several months, or even years, to studying and getting enough credits to get a license. For providers and caregivers looking to run their own homes, this could be a good fit. Investors, however, might not specialize in healthcare and have the needed certifications.

Which brings me to the next subject area: you'll need a strong passion for helping the elderly to get you through all the legwork involved with setting up and running a residential care home. That's because this type of business is really a lifestyle choice. You must be ready to jump up at 3:00 a.m. and arrange for a resident to be taken to the hospital if they wake up and have a medical emergency. You have to be ready to meet with families who are looking for a place for their elderly relative and can only come by to see you on a Saturday to talk about it. In other words, this isn't a DIY project you can do at your convenience. It's not a side hustle you can dedicate a few hours to each evening. And it's certainly not a nine-to-five job, which grants the luxury of clocking out at the end of the day and leaving all the looming to-dos for the next shift.

"Do you mean it's a nonstop commitment?" you might be asking. "What if I get a team of caregivers to oversee the needs of the residents? Won't I only have to devote a certain number of hours to my residential care home during the week?" These are good, valid questions. When people ask these exact things of me, I typically mention that it's really, really tough to go off duty if you start a residential care home on your own. There's a simple reason for this: ultimately, you're taking on numerous adults (usually between two and six) who need constant supervision. What do you do if a caregiver calls in sick? Someone has to take that shift. And that someone could be you if a backup employee isn't available. In addition, there are so many aspects that need overseeing in this line of work. Remember how we talked about the seniors' families? Those relatives also need your attention, and they must be communicated with and allowed to visit whenever they want. Then there are the service providers, like physical therapists, health aides, and landscaping companies that might be coming onto the property regularly. A typical day is full of activity and bustle from morning to night. And that is followed by another day of that same flurry of movement. As the owner of the residential care home, many responsibilities will naturally fall to you, and, literally, people's lives depend on you.

This is why, when answering these initial questions, I often add that you need to have the right personality for this type of investment. You'll want to care deeply for the well-being of others in general—and seniors especially—and have enough stamina to get through long days and ongoing tasks to manage. If you don't have the heart for it, others will notice right away. Residents might think you view them as a burden or grow concerned that you're only in the business to make money.

If they sense either of these things, even if they're not true, they might move to another place. Their families probably won't recommend your residential care home to others, which could hurt when you have spots to fill and would benefit from some positive word of mouth about your place. And while those are all negative factors, let's not forget the biggest downer of not having an innate desire to help the elderly. You simply won't be happy doing it. It will be really tough to stay motivated and work through the obstacles you'll encounter along the way. And that's no way to live your life.

Even if you have the real estate experience, healthcare expertise, and driving passion, there's still one hurdle to cross. That's the business concept I alluded to before. Taking a DIY approach to a residential care home is really a unique investment and business combination. You are dealing with two distinct segments. There's the real estate property investment itself and then the business as well. So you're managing a property while running a business.

Managing a property involves all the typical tasks: paying the mortgage and taxes, making sure everything inside is in good order, overseeing the interior design, and fixing any repairs. Many of these jobs seem pretty simple at first glance. And some of them are. But you have to remember you'll be keeping the property in nice shape while running a twenty-four-seven senior-care service. And as we just mentioned, this isn't an ordinary company; it's a full-time commitment that requires 110 percent dedication.

For the residential care home, you'll need a business plan, or at least some sort of manual to follow. No business is worth starting if you just open the doors and hope for the best: you must have some sort of financial guidance. How does McDonald's know what price to put on a burger? How do landlords decide what they will charge for rent for a two-bedroom apartment? Who makes sure the expenses are paid every month? I'm just showing you here that it can get complicated—quickly. If you don't have a plan or model to follow, you could be swimming in debt faster than I can say, "Is there anything I can help you with?"

Sure, in theory, anyone could draw up a plan, start a business, and be making money right away. But that's not how it usually works. In the United States, about half the businesses that open and hire employees will close within five years.[54] I don't mention this to be negative, but I think it's important to be realistic. And as the years pass, the statistics actually slope downward even more. Ten years after making their start, just a third of businesses in the United States remain open.[55] It might begin to look like you are lucky if you can keep operating for a couple of years, let alone five or even a decade.

The reasons that businesses shutter vary, but one of the main ones is this: the failure to deliver value. That whole concept of underpromising and overdelivering applies here. To succeed, it's much better to agree to certain terms with a resident and their family and then go above and beyond to deliver an outstanding service. For instance, if you say you provide outings for residents and then take them on excursions that are so meaningful to them that they can't wait to tell their families about the wonderful time they had, families will notice and applaud your efforts. Businesses that fail often do the exact opposite, which is overpromise and underdeliver. For example, don't guarantee organic meals and then open cans of generic meat and beans for a supper if you run short on funds one month. That sends the wrong message. It also might lead seniors and their families to believe you aren't caring for their overall health in the best possible way.

And even if you think you are providing value, you need to make sure the residents and their families view it that way too. In fact, you'll want families to consider your place to be better than others on the market. What if they don't see any advantage in moving their family member to your home, instead of an assisted-living facility? If they don't see the difference between your care home and a larger facility, they're not going to be ready to pay a monthly rent for your place, especially if it is the more expensive option.

There are other general reasons businesses fail, and it's worth pointing out a couple here. Some businesses can't create an effective sales funnel.[56] At a basic level, a sales funnel refers to every step someone must take to become your client.[57] It typically involves stages like making a potential client aware of your business, getting them interested in what you have to offer, encouraging them to consider the service, showing them just how your place is preferable to others on the market, and then, finally, enticing them to choose your business. In terms of residential care homes, if you don't have a great sales funnel in place, you won't be able to draw residents. And ultimately, having no residents means no revenue. I think you can see where I'm going with this. In short, it's a setup for fast failure.

To get that sales funnel, you'll need to be ready and willing to work with places that will help families find a home for their loved ones. Some of these places call themselves "referral agencies." They act like a middleman between you and the client. They fit in your sales funnel because they have access to many potential clients, they help spread awareness about your place, and they show potential clients what you have to offer. Those potential customers can then get in touch with you and decide to put their loved one in your home. I provide this type of service, and I always mention that this arrangement can bring benefits for everyone—the family, the provider, the caregivers, and the investors.

Even after initially bringing in residents, if you're not able to portray your place as authentic and transparent, they might run away soon. In fact, the lack of these characteristics is a key reason many residential care homes ultimately close.[58] Residents and their families will expect clear guidelines and agreements. They will then want to see everyone held accountable to those measures. If your place doesn't come across as one that is open, honest, and working for the best interests of its residents and their families, don't expect to see a large return on your investment.

Finally, many times businesses shut down for other financial reasons.[59] This can happen if the owner has poor management skills and just isn't able to keep track of all the expenses and revenue in an organized way. In these cases, the business owner usually doesn't have a firm grasp on how much cash is really coming in and going out, and ultimately comes up short on funds. Financial failure can also stem from a misaligned business plan. The plan might outline certain revenue expectations that simply aren't realistic or goals that can't be achieved. A money crisis can also come from overspending. Think putting down $10,000 for a single couch is a good idea? Maybe it is and maybe it isn't, but there are a lot of expenses that go into a residential care home. Many of them, like grocery purchases, might not seem like big costs at the time, but overall they add up. In a residential care home business, it's essential to have someone with a watchful eye, who is constantly tuned in to how those figures move, to avoid spending too much money too fast.

Based on the issues we just covered, I don't usually recommend that people go out and start a residential care home on their own without giving it much thought. That's because I like people and want to see them thrive. I would hate to see someone do minimal research and then try to start their own home only to get in way over their head and drown in financial obligations they can't get out of.

You see, this conversation we're having over coffee is one I've had a million times (OK, not a million, but you get what I mean). I've often talked to others who have seen the successful residential care homes I have created. They have come to me and asked for advice. I have always freely shared my knowledge, but over time I've learned that people who have only a little bit of experience and expertise in the areas I outlined are really at a disadvantage. I've watched them flounder in this business simply because they didn't have the right qualifications and tools at hand.

Based on these conversations and my own track record of outstanding homes, I have come across an investment model that I believe is easier, and more fulfilling, for everyone involved. I call this the investor approach. As I mentioned earlier in this chapter, this method focuses on working with a partner. By doing so, you can rely on someone who has all the needed expertise and experience to set up a successful business. You'll also be able to get those great investment returns much more readily and without having it consume your time twenty-four seven! We'll go over the main concepts of this approach in the next section.

THE INVESTOR APPROACH

As I mentioned earlier, here's a better idea: work with a partner when opening a residential care home. Think about it for a moment. Would you rather (a) learn by making mistakes, losing thousands of dollars (or more) during the process, and run the risk of completely losing your investment dollars with no return, or (b) put that money to work right away by giving it to someone who knows exactly what they are doing? It's pretty easy to see which path we should take.

But let's not jump to assumptions without laying out the facts. Here's a bit more of what I mean when I refer to the investor method: Through this approach, a partner will oversee the actual setting up and running of the residential care home. They'll take care of many things (or sometimes everything), from finding the property to getting it ready for guests to bringing in residents and then overseeing its daily operations. When bumps come up along the way, you won't have to worry about a thing, as your partner will smooth everything over. That said, we should note that a partner who really knows the field isn't likely to make too many missteps. Here I'm just referring to the natural setbacks and obstacles that come up over the course of any project. With a solid partner, these minor incidents can be worked through and overcome on a timely basis.

One great thing about working with a partner is that they can free up your time. Rather than being chained to the daily ins and outs of running a business and managing a property, you can pursue other activities and interests. Essentially, you can let your investment money do its work and expect financial gain while putting in very little effort on your end.

The beauty of this type of partnership is that it can be tailored to your needs and wants. For instance, you'll initially sit down with the partner and lay out your specific goals and ideas. The partner will work with you as you decide how much you want to invest and how involved you want to be in the investment itself. If you express that you want to take a hands-off approach (as in having the partner take care of absolutely everything), that can be arranged. If you want a deeper level of involvement or commitment, that can be set up too. It's really about creating an investment agreement that fits your exact situation and needs.

Whatever the specifics of the arrangement, keep in mind that while working with a partner, you'll still get that cash flow we mentioned. And this ongoing amount can even increase over time. We'll talk about that more in depth in Chapter 6, which lays out the investor approach in further detail.

Are you breathing a sigh of relief? Me too. Trust me, this investor approach is much easier. It takes a lot of the burden off your shoulders while still providing you that solid return. And by working with someone who is knowledgeable and experienced, those great investment benefits we listed will play out easily.

But before we move on to the next chapter, let's pause to take another sip of coffee and consider a few more perks. In addition to the time-saving and financial benefits, working with a partner means you don't have to become an expert in real estate. Remember how we mentioned that selecting the right property is a key element to a successful residential care home? It's much less stressful to leave those decisions to a partner who is well informed on the market and has experience buying and selling residential care homes.

You also won't have to become an expert in senior care. If you choose a partner who has a solid background in healthcare and, specifically, in working with seniors, the partner can handle the licensing requirements and certifications needed to get the place up and running. Aside from the logistics of senior care, that partner will be very tuned in to the emotional needs of families and residents. For instance, the process of relocating an aging parent to a place that offers higher levels of care is often fraught with tension. A partner will be accustomed to handling the stresses that both the parent and their adult children are feeling and will be able to help everyone adjust and find satisfaction with the new living situation. In fact, a great partner will help families and residents see that moving the senior into a residential care home was the best decision they could have made. I mention this here to show that you can depend on a partner to handle these types of emotionally charged situations, which naturally occur when working with seniors. You can lean on their expertise and let them take care of these steps.

A great partner will also be driven by a passion for helping the aging population and be eager to treat older adults as human beings with individual needs and rights. As we discussed previously, having that strong interest in caring for seniors really helps make the home a place where residents can thrive. This type of atmosphere is also one that families will see as valuable, which is a key trait that's needed for a residential care home to stay in business. Furthermore, a welcoming place focused on the seniors living there will be viewed as transparent and authentic, which are other essentials in the residential care business. Ultimately, happy residents help a place gain a great reputation; their satisfaction will also allow the business to grow and do well financially. This, of course, ultimately leads to more funds in your pocket.

Finally, a partner with great business sense, along with experience in running residential care homes, will enable your investment to reap ongoing, long-term financial gains. That's because the person you make an agreement with will understand how to set up a successful business plan and carry it out. They'll be in tune with rental rates and revenue expectations. They will know how to advertise the place, build an effective sales funnel, and generate income. They'll also be able to decipher and manage all the expenses involved with running the home, ranging from caregiver wages to supplies to groceries to home maintenance, and everything else needed to keep the business going on a day-to-day basis.

In the next chapter, Chapter 5, we'll look at how you can set up a residential care home on your own. As we've already mentioned, there are a lot of steps involved. In the following chapter, Chapter 6, we'll take a hard look at what it's like to invest in a residential care home with a partner.

If you're already thinking that you want to go with the investor approach, you may still find Chapter 5 helpful. It will give you a sense of the business side of residential care homes, and it will also help you understand the process involved in creating this type of senior care. Or you may just prefer to jump straight ahead to Chapter 6, where we will take a deep dive into the investor model to see what it's really like to work with a partner to invest in residential care homes. We'll also delve more fully into best practices for providers and caregivers.

The choice of which chapter to read next is yours, but whatever you do, stick around, because after we sort through these approaches, we're going to look at additional important elements like culture and work environments. At each step, you'll see how these different components come together to thrive under the residential care home model I've designed. I draw from my experiences and knowledge to create what I believe is a great place for seniors and everyone else involved. With that in mind, let's carry on to the next topics.

CHAPTER 5

————

The Do-It-Yourself Approach: The Challenges of Setting Up a Residential Care Business on Your Own

Before you think about opening the doors of a home to seniors, I have to warn you: expect to work. A lot. Setting up and running a residential care business is no small task, and it's generally a tedious undertaking that takes much longer than anyone plans for. I know this because I have developed and run many residential care homes myself—and I have watched others in my area try to set up and run a residential care home only to have it not work out according to plan. While I've refined my system along the way and been very successful, I'm here to say that it takes many, many steps to get this done.

To properly understand what type of investment we're talking about, and to give you an insider's look at how a senior home can be established, it's worth setting aside some time to examine a road map. Specifically, this road map will start at the very beginning of the process and lead you through all the steps needed to create and operate a residential care home. That means we have to initially look at how to round up the right real estate. We'll also go through the importance of making the home senior-ready, getting the right licenses and certifications, and then marketing the business. Finally, we'll peruse the art of bringing in residents and managing the place as a business. Are you tired yet? (Just kidding! But in all seriousness, you will be exhausted just thinking about the workload by the time we get to the end of each of the steps involved!).

We should make one final point before plunging in: think of this chapter as a behind-the-scenes glance at creating a healthy habitat for seniors. What I mean by that is, it's absolutely a must to set up a senior home the right way. As we've seen in the past few chapters, caring for the older generation is something I hold near and dear. I think it's essential to provide an environment that's caring, safe, and welcoming. After all, we've seen plenty of examples of how large systems can overlook individual needs and personal preferences. If everything is set up the right way, however, a residential care home will be a secure, regulated environment that feels like a home where seniors will thrive. Let's get started.

FINDING THE HOME

Browsing online for ten minutes and then making an offer on the first place you like is not the way to secure a solid residential care home and start your business. So what is? I'll tell you, but in order to do that, we have to step outside our own perspective. Rather than looking at homes to see what we like in them, we must approach this search from the senior's perspective as well as from their family's point of view.

I bring up the senior's perspective because, quite frankly, they are going to live in the residence. The home will need to be very comfortable, and it will need to accommodate them. And the family's view is important too. Remember how we talked about adult children taking steps to look out for their aging relatives? Those same people—the adult children—are going to be the ones looking for housing options when their loved one has to leave their current place of residence. Those family members—not the senior—will likely be the first ones to find and contact your residential care home.

Now think about this: Say you buy a place in a neighborhood in a downtown area that has the reputation of being dangerous because you love how the home looks and the price is right. Now pretend the families that will be most interested in your house all live in the suburbs. Don't expect them to be immediately attracted to your home. If they put their mom there, they'll have to drive an hour one way through heavy traffic every time they want to see her. And they might be scared to go there at night. Basically, it's not going to happen. They won't call you asking for a tour of the place after seeing the address.

You can see where I'm going with this. In real estate, you'll often hear the phrase "Location, location, location." Well, guess what? That saying applies directly to residential care homes. You can't have a place in a crowded metro area if you're trying to attract a small-town, quiet-neighborhood-loving clientele. You'll also want to avoid places on the other end of the extreme: a beautiful ranch house set in the rolling mountains of Montana, a.k.a. the middle of nowhere, is going to be hard for families in large cities to drive to on a regular basis.

For these reasons, you'll want a place that is easy to reach for the families who will want to visit their relatives. That's why you'll often find residential care homes located in areas where other families are living and making a place to call their own. This might mean a quiet neighborhood in the suburbs. Or it could mean a sector of a city that has a reputation for being family-friendly and safe. After all, you won't find many family members eager to place an aging dad in a neighborhood that is known for its high crime rates and deadly evenings on the streets.

They're going to want to put their parent in a place that looks secure, that feels safe, and that is easy for them to travel to every day, once a week, twice a month, or however often they'd like to visit.

In addition to finding a quiet, safe neighborhood that might be full of other families, you'll need to check and see if the property can be used for your residential care business. Many homeowners' associations (HOAs), for instance, will say no if you ask them for permission to turn a house in their zone into a residential care home. That's because HOAs typically have rules set up for the homes they oversee. They might have regulations indicating that no commercial businesses can be carried out on the properties within their zone. Since a residential care home includes a business that operates on the property—the senior-care aspect—those in charge might shake their heads if they hear of a senior home moving in.

Still, before you make a note to steer clear of HOAs and avoid them at all costs, I want to point out that there may be some exceptions. For example, you might try talking to those in charge of the HOA and explaining to them how you really want to help seniors. Or you might try negotiating a deal with them, such as offering residents who are part of the HOA a discount if they use your services. That sort of approach can open doors. For instance, there may be residents within the HOA who want a new place for their older parents and who would be thankful to have their parents close to their own home. You could end up befriending the HOA and even getting some of their regulations altered for your business. It is also important to point out to them that a residential care home is zoned as residential, not commercial. Now, that doesn't typically happen, and I'm not making any guarantees. I'm just saying that there could potentially be some flexibility within certain HOAs, depending on the area and who is in charge.

But you need to check on these things before you sign any real estate deals. You don't want to purchase a property and then realize it can't be used for a residential care business. If you take out financing to complete the deal, you could really be at a loss. You'll have a home that essentially needs to be kept as an investment or sold before it's had time to grow in value. This could set you back financially before you even start your residential care business!

And you shouldn't automatically think of turning your own place into a residential care home either. That's because the shape and form of the home matter—a lot. If you have a two-story home that was built in the early 1900s and you hang a "Residential Care Home" sign in your front yard, watch out. Your new senior residents might not even be able to climb the rickety, twisty steps to get to the front door, let alone scale the uneven stairs leading to the bedrooms on the upper floor. Even if the residents can walk and climb stairs, for safety reasons, they really shouldn't have to commit to climbing up and down those stairs every day for the next years of their life. They could get a serious injury just from getting out of bed and heading to breakfast. Or their health conditions could change and render them unable to walk, which would make maneuvering the stairs extremely challenging. In fact, your state's regulations for senior homes may prohibit staircases in the areas of the home where residents live.

The ideal residential care home is a one-story home, as this will avoid the necessity of asking the elderly people living in it to move up and down the stairs. If you have a place with two or three stories, you could end up with space that goes unused. That also becomes a loss, because you are paying for square footage that doesn't bring in revenue. Now, some families may decide to operate a residential care business on the first floor of a home and live on the second floor, but that will be a personal choice for you and your loved ones.

When you are thinking about the business aspects, you should plan on creating the home for seniors on just the ground floor. And one final note on the number of floors before we move on: don't plan on using a basement for residents. A typical basement with stairs leading down to it and very few windows won't be adequate for seniors. Now, there could be exceptions if the basement has a ground floor entryway and large windows, but speaking generally, you'll want to avoid using a basement for a senior home. You could possibly use the lower level of a home for storage or other purposes, just not the day-to-day senior-living activities.

Let's move on to the actual square footage of the home. You'll want to think about how big—or small—the home is so you can determine how many residents can live there. Say you buy a three-bedroom home with two bathrooms in a residential area. Are you going to house up to three residents and offer each senior a private room? If so, you need to think about the income that will generate. If those three pay $5,000 a month each, your maximum revenue would be $180,000 per year. If you plan to have two residents per room, you could have up to six residents. In this case, if everyone pays $5,000 each month, the maximum revenue would be $360,000 per year. See the difference?

Before you cram as many beds as you can into each room, however, you need to stop and think about the purpose of the home. First, you're not creating a place that is supposed to operate just like an assisted-living facility. In other words, you don't want a large-scale housing setup that is made for many residents. We're going for a small, homelike atmosphere. A cramped environment will not create that spacious, uncluttered feeling you want in a great home that seniors will enjoy.

And it's not just a matter of comfort: the state you live in may have a strong voice about the level of occupancy and the size of room required for one or two residents. Some states have specific laws that dictate the maximum number of residents that can live in a home. You might only be allowed to have six, for instance. If your business model works better with twelve residents, you'll have to think about purchasing two homes to use, rather than offering housing for twelve individuals under one single roof.

This brings us to the next consideration, which is that you may need to make changes to the home. In fact, nine times out of ten, you should expect that substantial remodeling will be necessary to get the place senior-ready. These changes may include:

- Adding bathrooms
- Putting in wheelchair-accessible ramps
- Widening doorways
- Replacing carpet with slip-free flooring
- Revamping bathrooms
- Making more bedrooms

In other words, get out your construction hat, because you are going to need a contractor and many hours of work to get that place the way you want it. While the examples listed above are pretty self-explanatory, let's take a closer look at a couple of these housing changes to see what we're talking about when we say "remodeling." We'll start with bathrooms and then touch on bedrooms as well.

I like to use the example of revamping bathrooms because it is often a top priority for seniors and their families. Also, some states will have specific requirements for what you need to include. For starters, the good news is that there are many senior-friendly features you can put in a bathroom today. The bad news is that most of them take a substantial amount of time to install, and some require a pretty hefty financial investment.

Take walk-in showers, for instance. You might find a lovely property with a beautiful bathroom that features a large tub. Now, maybe some residents will really want a bathtub. For convenience's sake and to be practical, however, a walk-in or wheel-in shower makes much more sense. You'll see these advertised in senior magazines and on TV. They are great because they take away the need for an older person to step up and over the bathtub when they are ready to bathe. There are also walk-in bathtubs and walk-in bathtub-showers, which give seniors even more options. Each of these, of course, comes with a price tag and specific installation requirements.

As you work to make maneuvering around a bathroom easier, you'll want to keep in mind that many seniors will want—or, more accurately, need—grab bars. These are extra railings that go on the bathroom walls. High-seat toilets, no-slide bath mats, and easy-to-reach sinks are also sought-after features in senior-ready bathrooms.

In addition to considering the bathrooms in the property you're looking to buy, you need to look at the number of residents you plan to accommodate. Then you'll have to evaluate how many bathrooms the home has and ask yourself if you are going to offer private bathrooms to each resident or not. If you do offer a private bathroom to every resident, you may have to add more bathrooms to the home. Private bathrooms could be an extra feature that some families might want and be willing to pay extra for. Or individual bathrooms might not be something that your target group of families wants to spend money on. It will be up to you to research this question (and, really, all other questions related to what families in your area are looking for).

Assessing the bedrooms in a potential residential care home is another major issue when it comes to prepping the property for residents. I noted this on the list of home remodels because it will always come up as a factor to consider when you turn a home into a residential care facility. You'll have to look at the number of bedrooms and decide if more are necessary. You'll also need to determine if the ones you have are large enough. Remember how we discussed pairing up residents and offering one room for two individuals? Even if this looks like a great part of your business plan on paper, it won't work if the bedrooms are so small that you can't possibly fit two beds into a single bedroom.

If you decide to add on a bedroom (or more than one) to the home, you might have to carry out a major remodel to turn certain spaces into bedrooms. Or you might need to expand the size of the home. This often entails a substantial addition. Bottom line: if you choose to include more bedrooms or to make the existing bedrooms bigger, you're usually looking at a significant construction project. You'll have to oversee the process and dedicate time to it.

If you hire a contractor to carry out bedroom adjustments or any other remodels, the easiest way to find someone to do the job—performing a quick Google search and grabbing a contractor's name from the results—is potentially the most hazardous. Let me tell you why: opting for just anyone to do major work on a home you are using as an investment holds many, many risks. They might do a mediocre job, or they could charge you through the roof, or they may ignore the city or state regulations. All of this means headaches for you and, more importantly, wasted time and money. After a bad experience with one contractor, you'll often have to go about finding someone else who will do the job the right way. By the time you finish, you might be thousands of dollars over budget.

You need to find someone who is trustworthy, is fair, and comes highly recommended. If you don't have people to ask for referrals, you're in trouble. Even if you do have access to referrals, you'll want to interview several options. Invite contractors to come and assess the projects you want done. Ask them for a quote and present a few more questions, just to see how they are as a person and what projects they have already carried out. You'll want to hire someone with experience, who offers a fair price, follows all codes, and agrees to the terms you lay out.

As you can see, a lot of work is involved! Are you ready for a break? I hope not, because we are just getting started. After finding the property and getting it ready, we need to move on to the next step. This involves licensing the home and getting it prepped to operate as a business.

LICENSING REQUIREMENTS

No, this does not mean you have to go to the DMV to get a license. (That's just a joke—I thought you could use a mood breaker by now, after all that humdrum real estate talk!) And it doesn't even mean you need to simply fill out some paperwork (though you will definitely have papers to sort through and sign as part of this step!). Here we are referring to getting the right licenses to be able to operate a residential care home in your particular region.

Notice I say region, and by that I mean you'll need to abide by the laws in the city and state where you live. We won't talk about the specifics for all fifty states, as each state has its own set of licensing requirements for those who want to start a senior home. And we won't cover city codes, though many localities will have their own requirements for businesses.

One important factor to bear in mind here, as we talk about licenses, is that laws can change. This is true in a general sense, but for our discussion, it is especially relevant in the senior-care space. This is because the older population is growing, as we noted in previous chapters, and states are having to deal with an aging demographic. I don't say that in a derogatory way; I'm simply indicating that states are naturally going to continue looking for ways to make sure seniors are accommodated and in safe environments. In legal terms, this means changes may be made to state laws that reflect this trend and help provide safety measures for the elderly. When it comes to getting licenses for a residential care home, you won't want to rely on what you see in outdated pamphlets or online material. It's best to contact your state and local authorities to learn about the latest guidelines.

While these regulations vary, let's go through a few examples so you can better understand the work required to get the licenses you need. Some states will want you to have spent a certain number of hours caring for seniors before you can get a license to run a residential care home. In the state of Washington, the requirement is a thousand hours of senior care.[60] In other states, you'll need to complete a course on senior care that could involve a hundred hours or more. Some states will ask that you hire a licensed nursing-home administrator.[61] If you live in one of these states, that means you'll need to either become a licensed nursing-home administrator yourself or find someone who is and bring them on board. You'll also need to check if the nursing-home administrator license needed for residential care homes is the same as what is required for nursing homes there, or if there is a difference.

The licensing process can be long and tedious. In addition to dedicating hundreds or, more likely, thousands of hours to get the certifications you need, you can expect to get inspected. The state will want to see your home before you begin operations to make sure everything is in line with the law. And keep in mind that the law is detailed. The fire code might require a path, accessible to all residents, leading from the inside of the home to a safe place outside, in case they need to quickly exit the building due to a fire or other hazard. You might have to widen hallways and doorways to accommodate wheelchairs. And some regulations—like the fire ones—you will still want to follow even if the state doesn't require them to provide a safe environment for future residents.

HIRING CAREGIVERS

Residential care homes require someone to be available on a twenty-four-seven basis to care for the seniors who live there. This means that if you plan to do it all on your own, you'll need to be available all day, every day, to care for your residents. Doesn't sound like a feasible solution to you? You're right. It's not.

Instead, you'll need to hire workers to help. If you've been thinking that it is relatively easy to secure the right property and set up a senior home, here's where it gets really tricky. When you're hiring people, you won't want just anybody tending to your residents day in and day out. These caregivers will be your frontline workers and will have constant contact with your residents. You'll want to keep those residents safe, happy, and comfortable, and the interactions they have with caregivers are very important when it comes to meeting these goals. Furthermore, your region may have specific codes regarding caregivers—like we saw in the previous section with the example of some states requiring a licensed nursing-home administrator to be in charge.

As a starting point, here's an overview of what you'll want to think about when you are first setting up a worker plan for your residential care home:

- Caregiver certifications
- Caregiver wages
- Caregiver benefits
- Opportunities for raises
- Contracts
- Caregiver experience
- Caregiver personality

Let's go over each of these briefly, starting with certifications. You'll have to check with your state to know what sort of training your caregivers need. Some common requirements are a basic caregiver certification, certified nursing assistant (CNA) certification, home health aide (HHA) certification, CPR certification, and dementia-care certification. Needless to say, you don't want to put someone on payroll that doesn't have the right initial qualifications.

You also must think about how much you'll need to pay the caregivers. If you offer low wages compared to the market rate in your area, you might have more turnover than you want. If you offer higher-than-average wages, you could attract high-quality workers. Whatever strategy you use will ultimately have a big impact on your cash flow.

Furthermore, pay is something you'll need to research before you make any decisions. We just touched on lower-than-average and higher-than-average wages, but that implies that you know what the average rates are in your area. If you're not aware of the average caregiver rates in senior homes and care facilities, you'll have to first investigate in your area. In addition, since you'll (ideally) be paying these caregivers through the revenue that you bring in, you'll need to understand how much revenue you're expecting each month from residents.

This, of course, refers back to that business plan we mentioned. As an example, say your home can fit up to three residents who pay $5,000 each month. You'll bring in $15,000 over a one-month period when the home is fully occupied. If you pay more than that in caregiver wages, you'll be in the red right away.

Besides a paycheck, what else are you going to offer caregivers? Will you provide them with meals, give them vacation days, or offer health insurance? Benefits such as these must be considered before you begin a discussion with a potential candidate. You don't want to be caught talking to someone who has questions about benefits that you're unable to answer. Also, if you offer benefits that are too generous, you won't be able to bring in a profit. In the end, if the business loses too much money, you won't be able to keep caregivers. You can see why this is an important aspect to figure out before you start placing job ads.

Offering caregivers the option of a raise is another critical element that has a fine line. Provide little or no chance of a wage increase, and workers might not be happy. Put too much on the table, and you could end up in a tight spot, financially speaking. For those doing this for the first time, it can be really hard to know what a good raise is. It can also be tough to estimate how this will affect cash flow.

When bringing in employees, you can't just shake hands with workers and agree to pay them every two weeks. You'll need contracts, complete with all your guidelines and policies. This should include well-established expectations for the caregiving work. It will also lay out consequences for unfulfilled commitments. If you don't have clearly laid-out terms, you could find yourself in a tough position if a caregiver isn't performing to your expectations. You might not be able to let that person go if certain repercussions are not written out in the form of a signed contract.

And one more thing about contracts: they will need to meet all state and federal employment requirements too. This means you could be spending a hefty number of hours prepping those documents or paying high fees to have a legal expert do it for you. Bottom line: when you bring on workers, you'll need to make agreements that they can sign before they start.

This brings us to the end of the bullet-point list I provided, but I have to warn you there's much, much more to the hiring process than first meets the eye. Consider this step: the interview. Take my word for it when I say you shouldn't just ask a few lighthearted questions and then base your decision on the potential worker's answers. Even if those first questions spark a nice discussion, keep in mind that these workers will spend a lot of time with your residents. You'll need to ask in-depth, insightful questions to determine if they will make a solid contribution to your business.

Before you carry out an interview, remember that older residents in your home might not have the mental capacity, due to a disability such as dementia, to stand up and defend themselves. In fact, they'll need someone who will take care of and stand up for them. During the interview process, you'll want to find out if a caregiver has a passion that runs deep enough to take on this responsibility. You'll be interested in having someone who will look out for the senior's rights, health, and well-being. To learn if a candidate is up to the task, you can bring up questions that touch on the caregiver's past experiences with the elderly, what responsibilities they feel are necessary for the job, why they want the job, and what type of environment they think is needed in order for seniors to thrive. In other words, enough questions to learn a bit about their personality and see if they have the passion and drive needed for the job.

Here's one last tidbit to keep in mind when hiring caregivers: you'll have to compare the caregiver-to-resident ratio required by your state to what you plan to offer. For instance, let's say your state requires one caregiver to be present if there are six people in the home. Are you going to provide more than that minimum, such as two caregivers for six residents? If you do, it will affect the number of caregivers you need to hire. It will also influence the total amount you need to spend on wages (e.g., paying two caregivers rather than one).

In conclusion, hiring the absolute minimum number of workers and providing the lowest-possible wages may be appealing from an initial cost perspective. But you need to ask yourself, "Is this what I really want to offer?" If you want a place with high-quality care that outshines the competition, that's sustainable, and that is truly seen as a haven, you'll want to go above and beyond. That's the philosophy I've always instilled and carried around, and it has done me, my workers, and the residents and their families good. We'll get to more of that in a later chapter.

FURNISHING SUPPLIES

You'll need a lengthy list of supplies to maintain the home, keep it clean, and allow caregivers to carry out their jobs. When I started my first residential care business, I knew I would have to purchase everything for the house, from paper towels and napkins to shampoos, soaps, and creams to cleaning supplies and so on. Talk about a lot of trips to the stores and researching suppliers to find the best deals and quality! Stocking up is not at all like taking a weekly run to the grocery store. You have to think through every item and how much of it you'll need. The exact amount you'll have to have on hand will be based on the number of individuals living in the home.

Now, here's a caveat: you'll find that some residential care homes ask seniors to bring in their own supplies, or at least a portion of the items they'll need. Others will have a separate charge that they ask seniors to pay to cover the supplies. If you make seniors bring in some items or charge them separately for these items each month, that will be your choice. I'm here to say, however, that it is much, much easier to include this expense in the overall rent that residents pay. Which means, of course, you'll need to know how much supplies cost and factor that into your overall rent.

Just as you'll want to consider the level of service you'll be providing when you add caregivers to your staff, it's essential to think through all the supplies you'll include. Will you buy the generic brand for everything? Will you offer higher-quality products that might be more expensive to get? For many items, it can be advantageous to buy in bulk. This requires spending some time looking for suppliers to buy from locally or online. You might decide to become a member at a place like Costco or Sam's Club, which cater to small businesses and the supplies they need. All of this requires some up-front legwork.

At the beginning, it may be difficult to know how often you'll need to make repurchases. How long will a large pack of paper-towel rolls last? How many boxes of toothpaste will be needed for a month? You'll be making some initial guesses as you start out.

Over time, you can set up a system that lays out all the supplies that are actually being used in your home. You might have caregivers notify you or mark a chart to let you know when supplies need to be refilled. You can also develop a budget and then watch for sales. I often take advantage of steep discounts and use the opportunity to stock up, so the residential care homes never run short. This method also provides an overall savings on the cost of the items needed.

A major expense when it comes to residential care home supplies is often the food. Of course your residents will need to eat every day, and their nutrition will play a big role in their overall health. Your meal-related expenses can vary greatly, depending on the residents' diets, the type of groceries you purchase, and where you shop. This becomes plain if you tour different care homes. You may come across some that are looking to cut costs and thus regularly serve cheaper items like generic hot dogs to their residents. Higher-end places will often include menus with more vegetables and fewer processed foods. In the homes I've overseen, we've always specialized in organic foods, and I've never offered anything to residents that I wouldn't have served my own family or guests. It's just that simple.

If you opt for a strategy that focuses on high-quality foods, you'll typically have a substantial food bill as a result. Keep in mind, however, that you need to remember the whole picture when figuring out food. Residents who are well nourished and healthy and enjoy mealtimes will likely stay longer. Thus, by serving better food, you'll increase the average length of a resident's stay. You'll also naturally bring in more business by building a reputation for having nutritious food consistently available to guests. My advice here: don't shortchange yourself, or others. Avoid those super-cheap packs of bologna and keep everyone's stomachs and hearts happy by reaching for high-quality meats, cheeses, fruits, and vegetables.

MARKETING EFFORTS AND WOES

We saw in earlier chapters that there are a growing number of older citizens in the United States. Given this, you might think that, with so many elderly folks out there, bringing in those first residents will be a piece of cake. I'm here to warn you that such a mindset is completely wrong. Understand that marketing will be an ongoing process, and an especially steep hill to climb when you are first opening your doors.

It's not hard to see why: put yourself in the shoes of someone who is looking for a place for their elderly aunt. Where should their beloved auntie go? To a new place in town that no one has heard about? Probably not. To a spot they see online that has zero reviews? Definitely not.

Now pretend you've set up your residential care home and are hoping to get some residents for it, but you have no leads. No one in your area knows about it, you haven't done any advertising, and while you have it listed online, there aren't yet any reviews.

In this scenario, that family with the elderly aunt might end up choosing a large facility over your residential care home. Here's why: they don't hear anyone besides you recommending that they use your residential care home, and they don't see any online reviews about it. As a result, they have no idea what it is really like. They are very concerned about their dear aunt's well-being, and they don't want to test out a new care service by using her as a guinea pig. They do know, however, that they want every place they consider to be dependable and trustworthy. That's why, in their search, they might settle on a nursing home that has been around for decades but has an average review of 3.5 out of 5 stars. Sure, it doesn't get great reviews, they think, but compared to zero reviews, they decide to opt for an average place that seems stable over a nice-looking place with no background.

This is one of the reasons why you won't typically see a brand-new residential care home, if it's being started by someone who is doing it for the first time, fill to capacity as soon as it opens its doors. The opposite is more realistic. It's not unusual for a residential care home to go for six months, or even a year, before getting its first resident. If this happens to your residential care home, remember that you could be spending money—and quite a bit of it—on advertising with no revenue coming in.

As I related earlier, I do help with referrals to fill homes. That said, it's important for me to know the providers of the places I recommend to families. I only send elderly folks to homes that I have vetted and believe will be a perfect fit for them.

And don't forget, even if it is difficult to find residents, there will still be a home to care for. You can expect to be responsible for covering the following costs while you wait for residents:

- Mortgage
- House maintenance
- Home repairs
- The caregivers you hire, depending on the agreement you make with them
- Property taxes

Since you are operating this home as a business, you'll have to think about cash flow. How will you pay for those expenses if you have no residents—and thus no revenue—for several months, or even a year or longer?

Even though it's tough to gather those first residents, the right marketing tools can make it easier to fill a home. While going over all the best advertising strategies would require another book (!), I will cover a few of the most important marketing activities to carry out here. Keep in mind that these are just a few strategies, and the exact ones you choose will depend on your location and situation.

First and foremost, you need to set up a website. After all, how else are people going to find you? Certainly not just by driving by. In fact, some neighborhoods won't allow you to put a sign in front of the place indicating that it is a residential care home. This means that setting up a website should be your first step (although by all means, put that sign up if it is allowed!).

As you put together your website and add content to it, you'll want to either use search engine optimization (SEO) or hire someone who can implement it. Basically, SEO refers to the process of making your site more visible when people perform searches related to your area or business.[62] For instance, say you live in Lexington, Kentucky. You might name your residential care home "Residential Care Home of Lexington, Kentucky" and then incorporate those words into the site. Including phrases like "residential care home" and "Lexington, Kentucky" in the pages will help. SEO is best done in a certain way (there are books written on this too!), so having professional help could make a big difference.

Making an easy-to-find, attractive website is key in today's world: families will usually start trying to find a new living situation for their aging relative by looking online. You don't want them to search on Google and then have your residential care home appear on page 23 of the search results. They'll never get to your place. They'll be too busy sifting through the senior-housing options in the top search results. And if they see other sites that look professional and are offering to care for their parent before visiting your page, which appears to have been put together by someone who was blindfolded (by which I mean it doesn't look good!), you can guess where they will go. That's right: to the other site, which has clean lines and solid formatting.

Which brings me to another must-have about your website: fill it up with pictures of your place—and make those photos count. Just as you'll want the site to come across as professional and serious, it's essential that the images you choose look outstanding. If you don't know anything about lighting and arranging, don't trust yourself to snap a bunch of shots and then load them to your site. You'll likely need to hire a professional photographer who knows what they're doing. The reason for this is pretty straightforward: you want the family member who is browsing your site to say, "Wow, that looks really bright and cheerful, and perfect for Uncle Gerald!"

In addition to creating a website, you can create a hands-on experience for people who are interested in checking out the home as an option. There are a couple of ways to do this. One method is to have an open house before you start welcoming any residents. This gives you a chance to showcase the amenities and give visitors a firsthand glimpse of what life would be like for their loved one. You could advertise the open house on your website and also pay for other ads about it. Another strategy would be to individually invite visitors to come and walk through the home. This might work well if someone calls you and asks about the place. You can offer them a chance to see the home for themselves and get a feel for the environment.

We've briefly touched on the topic of working with referral agents. It's worth bringing them up again here because they allow you to list your home on other websites that help connect families with residential care homes. Typically, these agents offer to help bring you residents and often charge you a fee (such as the first month's rent) for each resident that comes your way through them. I have a system for this, and it works well for individuals who have successfully set up a great home for seniors (which, as I've stated, is not easy to do!).

The goal of all these methods is the same: to pique interest and get visitors to walk through the doors of your residential care home. For this reason, you'll want to ensure the place is ready for their arrival. This means that the home must be tidy and that everything looks clean, bright, and refreshing. Put a vase of fresh flowers on the kitchen table, get some bread baking in the oven, or go through the flower beds outside and give them a thorough pruning. These steps are fairly similar to what you would do if you were trying to sell your own home. Just as you would do everything possible to give potential home buyers a great first impression, you'll want to give potential clients an initial experience they can't forget—in a good way, of course. You'll hope that they see a place that looks so great they are ready to sign a lease before leaving.

All of this, of course, means more work for you. If you can't do it yourself, you might hire a professional cleaning company or bring in a gardener for the yard work. You could ask a designer for input on colors and furniture arrangements. Overall, you'll want to do everything within your reach to make the place stand out when visitors arrive.

In addition to making the home look great, there is some paperwork that's worth preparing before an open house. For example, it's a good idea to put out information on a table or shelves where it can easily be seen. This might consist of a brochure featuring menu details, explanations of daily activities, a list of available excursions, and other services. Be careful not to overpromise here: you can't boast that you have "outings every Friday" if you plan to take seniors out twice a month. Residents and family members will quickly see the disconnect between the promise of the brochure and the reality of the home environment. And trust me, they will walk away—fast—if they see that inconsistency. They might even advise their friends to stay away too.

Let's run through one more marketing issue that will come up in your business plan before we move on: the price point. You will want to set a monthly rate for residents that they (or their families, or whoever is paying) can easily afford. At the same time, you need an amount that is high enough to cover all your expenses. Bear in mind that these expenses can pile up during a resident drought (by a "resident drought," I mean times when you have one or more available spots for residents that aren't being filled). You'll also have to think through how much you are going to charge people over time. For instance, are you going to start out with a low monthly fee that then increases every year? If you do, be aware that some families might not be happy paying more in the coming years. Or will you keep a consistent monthly rent for the entire time the resident lives at the home? This might be more appealing to families, but it will also mean you'd better know your numbers. Bottom line: you'll have to make sure your cash flow is sufficient to cover ongoing expenses, during both times of full occupancy and times of resident drought.

I don't mean to set a sad tone here with marketing issues, but I feel it's important to share these matters because I've watched other residential care homes fail. People have tried, often with the best intentions, to start a residential care home, but they just weren't able to bring in the residents they needed to cover the ongoing expenses. Or they didn't have their business model set up to be able to weather long periods of resident droughts, and eventually they ran out of cash and closed their doors. While it is hard to think about, this is a business, and bankruptcy is a real thing. It doesn't take much for someone to have to shutter a home and move on. This is especially true in today's world, where family members are going to be extra cautious about the health and safety measures that are being taken for their loved ones.

While it's a tough market, it's not impossible to navigate if you have the right expertise and experience. I built my business in a way that made it easy to get referrals. I now work with investors, providers, and caregivers to make sure seniors have a safe place where they can thrive. Those who come to me are generally impressed with the results they see. My point here, however, is that it is not simple to set up a senior-ready home. It takes a deep investment of time and commitment to make it happen.

MAINTAINING THE BUSINESS

When you get your first residents, you might be ready to jump up and down (I'll jump along with you, because let's face it, we just saw that getting those initial residents is a big task). OK, now it's time to move on, because the real work is only just beginning.

When families initially place a loved one in a residential care home, those family members will expect to receive the rules and regulations of the home. You should have all this information ready for them. The exact documents you'll need will vary from state to state. Generally speaking, the written documentation consists of information on the home, care guidelines, family-visiting and -involvement explanations, and emergency protocol. There will be a contract to sign too. In Washington, families also receive a list of their rights and an admission agreement, among other documents.

Generally speaking, to accept an initial client, there is an enormous amount of paper preparation that needs to be done. If you're bringing in a resident for the first time, plan to spend hours getting everything ready. You could also consider hiring a professional or legal expert to help you, but that will be another expense you'll have to factor into the total costs of running the home.

Also keep in mind that during this process of going over paperwork with the family and signing contracts, emotions will likely be running high. Listen to what June,[63] who had to put her terminally ill husband in a residential care home, said about the experience of having to admit she couldn't care for him at home any longer. "It just got too bad," she said. "I never thought it could get that bad. I thought I would be able to take care of him until he died."[64] If you're running a home on your own, you'll need to be prepared for highly stressed family members. They are often going through a difficult time, and their words and tone may come across as very tense. You'll want to show empathy and be ready to listen. You'll also need to be ready to calm any storms and help restore peace in the family. It's just part of this line of work.

Once you have residents in your care home, everything suddenly intensifies. There's the pressure to keep supplies stocked and not run out of anything; the need to always have caregivers (and top-notch workers, as we mentioned); the constant communication with family members; the overseeing of activities and excursions; the ongoing effort to maintain the home; the coordinating with healthcare services that might drop by to visit residents; the supervision of doctor visits; the management of unplanned events like COVID; and on and on. And then there is one guideline to prioritize above all these other practices. I'm referring to the fact that it's absolutely vital to keep residents well cared for and happy.

If you don't make sure residents have a warm, loving environment right from the beginning when they enter the home, don't be surprised if their family soon moves them elsewhere. And if they leave, your revenue will drop without residents (as we explained earlier), and it could be extra tough to fill their spot if the family writes a poor review of your place online where other potential clients can read it . . . see where I am going? Your business could collapse before you have time to say, "We'll work on having a better atmosphere with the next residents."

From my experience, you'll have a profitable operation if you make the well-being of residents your top priority. To do this, you need to make sure everything about the care home runs smoothly, of course. The lawn will need to be mowed, the food prepared consistently, the caregivers supervised, the paychecks distributed, the taxes paid, and the front doors fixed, in addition to everything else involved with maintaining a property that holds both a home and a business.

One more note before we move on: stay above the law. Perhaps this is a given, but it's worth emphasizing here, simply because I've watched what can happen when people try to cut corners while running a residential care home. They might not pay attention to changes in the state's licensing requirements. As soon as they get inspected, however, they have to shut down because they aren't following the codes in place.

Occasionally you see news headlines noting extreme cases of not following rules in care homes. One such instance occurred in Puyallup, Washington, when an elderly woman fell inside a residential care home and the caregivers didn't attend to her needs right away. Several days later the resident died. Officials arrested two individuals associated with the home, and the state suspended the home's state license so it could no longer operate. The other residents who had been in the home were moved elsewhere.[65]

That is an extremely sad story, and certainly it is the exception rather than the norm. But I feel it is worth including here, even though it breaks my heart to think about it, because it shows just how important it is to properly maintain these homes. It's essential to ensure that the care provided within their walls is always high-quality. It's easy to see why: people's lives are at stake. Even in situations that are not so extreme, the state will readily remove a license if authorities see that regulations are not being followed.

That's why, after your initial setup, you'll need to keep paying attention to those state requirements, because they can, and do, change from time to time. If your state sends out occasional updates or information on residential care home regulations, sign up to receive these updates. You might be able to get email notifications or texts that inform you of the latest amendments in laws or new regulations in your particular state and area. Also look for ways to network with other residential care home operators or local senior organizations. By doing so, you'll be able to hear about and stay on top of any changes as they occur. Staying well informed and up-to-date may mean the difference between a high monthly income and no business at all.

EXPANDING THE BUSINESS

While I think it's important to recognize the vast amount of work that is required to set up and start a residential care home, I want to include one more key consideration to this whole DIY approach before we move on and look at the advantages of working with a partner for the process. When we talk about setting up residential care homes, we don't mean to imply that all those building efforts stop after you create one initial home. There may—or may not—be opportunities to expand the business.

Take a moment and think of a residential care home like a small business. Now consider the following example. Say a doughnut store starts out in a commercial center. The owner runs the shop for several years or decades, and the small company does well. The owner makes enough money during that time to buy a nice little home for themselves and save enough to have a modest nest egg. Eventually, the owner wants to retire. They decide to sell the business to the next owner and settle into their long-awaited retirement. That's one scenario for a small-business operation.

But there is another, more exciting possibility: What if that doughnut shop starts out as a small place in a commercial center but does really, really well? Let's say it does so well that the owner decides to start another doughnut shop on the other side of town. And that one sells lots of pastries too, which leads the owner to expand to three shops. And then even more shops. In this example, the owner will have opportunities to bring in even more cash and probably have a nicer home than the single-shop owner. Their nest egg might get so big they can have a second home in retirement or do some global travel. When they want to sell the place, which has now grown to be a chain of doughnut stores, they can put a high price tag on it.

The same is true for residential care homes. Maybe you won't be setting up homes around the country (though it's not bad to think big), but keep in mind that I noted millions of people are going to need help in the coming years. Plenty of families will be looking for a place for elderly folks. We also looked at the need to make sure the residential care home is a place where seniors can thrive. In theory, then, setting up a good residential care home that is well liked could lead to the chance to start another one. You might create the second one in a nearby neighborhood or city. Then if you fill up your first residential care home with residents, you can refer those who express interest in the place to your second residential care home, where there may be an opening.

Like everything else, expanding by opening more residential care homes is not a piece of cake. It is a long, tedious process. Furthermore, it may not even be legally possible, depending on where you live. Let me explain: in some states, you might only be able to own and operate one home. This means you, on your own, would not be able to open a second one under your same name. You'll have to do the research in your area and ask local officials about the rules.

Let's pretend, for a moment, that you're able to open a second residential care home. The good part about this opportunity is that you've already been through everything the first time. You probably used that experience to learn and better understand the business. Doing the same steps for a second time is bound to be easier. You will be more familiar with the right real estate location, the type of remodeling you'll need to put in, and how to bring on caregivers and stock up on the right supplies.

Suppose things continue to go well and you decide to purchase even more properties and turn them into residential care homes. You may find that you can streamline some operations. For instance, you can use the same types of gardens for all of them, the same comfortable furniture, the same family-communication guidelines, the same bathroom fixtures, and so on. You can call on the same providers and suppliers for the different homes.

All this streamlining has a twofold benefit. First, you save yourself a bunch of work. Once you develop a menu for one place, for instance, that same menu could be used in all the homes. The same is true for that essential employee handbook. No need to sit down and write another one when you open your second or third residential care home. Just find the one you created for your first home and hit Copy. The second benefit lies in increased buying power. You could reduce your expenses if you buy in bulk, since you may be able to get better discounts and deals as you scale the business. You'll also, as in the doughnut-shop example we looked at that grew into a chain, have the chance to bring in more revenue. Overall, these steps increase your cash flow and generate higher profits.

Earlier in this chapter, we discussed the difficulty of filling up your first home. If you get residents for that first home, however, and build up a reputation of running an outstanding place for seniors, it could be easier to fill up the second place (especially if you work with me for those referrals!). That's because you'll have established yourself in the community and can draw on resources like good reviews from the first place to bring in more guests to the second home. This process could reduce the effort that is needed to market the second place.

In summary, in this chapter we walked through the steps of starting and potentially growing a residential care home. We saw how it's a solid business opportunity. I think it's pretty clear by now, however, that an immense amount of work and specific skill sets are needed to really get these homes off the ground and running. That's why it's worth looking at another approach to this type of investment. In the following chapter, we'll go over how to set up a residential care home with the help of a partner. We'll talk about how a partner can reduce your workload while simultaneously getting you a better return on the investment. Ready to jump in? Me too. Let's read on.

CHAPTER 6

How to Work with a Partner for a Residential Care Home

Tired of hearing how hard it is to get a residential care home up and running? Then I have great news: we're about to see how it can get easier. And better. There is a simpler way to start a residential care home, with less effort and less experience required. Let's not forget, as I alluded to earlier, that there is another strategy to potentially get an excellent return and be happy with your investment. The first step on that path involves creating a partnership. Once you've done that, your partner will handle a lot of the logistics, as they'll have the experience and expertise to do it well.

You may be wondering, "What exactly do you mean by a partnership?" If so, I have more great news. I think it's important to explain what I mean by partnership and how it plays out in this space. In real estate and investments, as you might know, it's not uncommon to work with others, and everyone plays a role. In this chapter, I'll go over the definition that we'll use to describe a partnership for a residential care home. I'll also share why you'll find that I, Nelly, can be that ideal partner. As we go through the various aspects, I'll list the attributes that the person should have, just in case you decide to look for this assistance on your own. (Keep in mind that I have been in this industry for a long time, created a successful business model to follow, and literally wrote the book on it! But I digress—let's continue our chat so I can answer some of the main questions that might be running through your head right now.)

A DEEP DIVE INTO PARTNERSHIP

So far, we've looked at the need in the United States for senior care. We've covered how residential care homes can help seniors thrive and be a great real estate investment. I've discussed how to set one up and run it on your own—and how hard and challenging that can be. Now, let's look at what happens when you add a partnership.

When you work with a partner, you free up your time and gain valuable help on the project. To be clear, in this book, when I mention a partner, I am referring first and foremost to myself, because you'll soon see why choosing me, with my unique skills and experience, is the route to go. (See my contact information in the back of the book and reach out! You'll also find a list of references there to help you on your journey from start to finish.)

Here's a quick take on why you'll want to make a partnership with me. I've seen so much in this industry over the years, and I have a lifelong passion that makes me always want to see seniors well cared for and in an environment that suits their needs. I've worked as a provider, a caregiver, a manager—and the list goes on—for around two decades. I have been in different medical facilities, including emergency rooms, hospitals, assisted-living centers, and nursing homes. In addition to having so many roles and working at all those places, I've even created and run my own residential care homes! And really, my experience goes back to my early childhood, when I helped my grandmom, which makes it almost a lifetime that I've been involved in senior care.

Looking beyond the medical, provider, and caregiving background (which is extremely important!), I have vast experience in other key areas. I have bought and sold many homes and have used my real estate insight to spot the best properties for this type of investment. I have also worked as a general contractor, so I know what it's like to remodel places and get them ready for seniors. I am not only familiar with running and managing construction projects but also aware of the steps needed to furnish the home so it is senior-friendly and also optimally appealing to high-end paying clients and their families. In short, I am everything you would want in a partner.

Let's use the next sections to go over the stages that I will lead you through as a partner. They start with choosing the real estate and then move on to getting the property ready and finishing the home. The final part consists of licensing and running the business the right way, making sure seniors are comfortable, safe, and fulfilled. As you read, you'll be able to imagine how this partnership can bring mutual benefits. And if you decide to go with someone else or have expertise in several of these areas and opt to try them on your own, use the characteristics listed as examples of what you'll want to have. Finally, bear in mind that I'm providing an overview here. When you contact me, we can set up a time to talk and go over the details of our specific arrangement to make sure it's a great fit for everyone involved.

GETTING THE REAL ESTATE

Like so many things related to business and investing, it's really about location! Location! Location! As we've seen, a profitable residential care home needs to be on the right property and in a well-suited neighborhood. This often means a residential area, where the streets are quiet and the lawns are well trimmed. If the location is beautiful, it will be more attractive to families who want a place that seems like a nice spot for their loved one. In my experience, seniors who live in lovely homes surrounded by an extensive landscape and nestled in a pretty part of town have a wonderful opportunity to thrive. And their relatives will likely be comfortable and feel that they made the right choice in placing their loved one in a great residence.

Whenever I search for the right location to set up a residential care home, there are always some features I look for, including making sure it is close to a hospital, main road, and emergency-care facilities. This is crucial, as you'll remember that quick access to healthcare is vital for a senior's medical conditions and quality of life. Getting a property that is close to these amenities enables the residents to get treatment right away if they need it. I also identify areas where ambulances can easily find and get to the home, which is important in times of need. Since I like to have service professionals visit the seniors, they should be able to navigate the roads and arrive at the property too. Some of these professionals include nail stylists, physical therapists, visiting nurses, and other medical assistants. These are just a few of the many features I search for in a location.

I also check for properties that are easy to convert into a senior-friendly home. If the house is great but it would be very hard to make changes to it, the costs for remodels could be steep. Up-front expenses that are simply too high will make it tough to run a business and come out ahead.

Being a real estate agent myself and having run my own residential care homes, I find it easy to walk through a place and imagine ways to remodel and make changes so that the residential care home can be as accommodating as possible to seniors. Now, if you're also an agent or have been involved in real estate investments, you may be familiar with going out to view properties and finding the right one too. You'll also know that there are usually many elements to consider in choosing the property that best fits your long-term goals.

While I have ample experience in this process and enjoy helping others, I also recognize that you may want to do this part on your own—especially if you have purchased property in the past or worked in this space. For these reasons, in this section I've listed the attributes to look for as you search for the right place. And remember, you can always contact me for a consultation or partnership in which you choose the real estate and I help you set up other parts of the business where you may not have as much experience (or the time needed to oversee everything, which can add up fast).

With that in mind, here are a few more quick tips I've learned during my career that I'll share before we move on. I know how to spot—and avoid—overpriced properties. I've also found ways to discover what might be a hidden gem—properties with great potential, like a beautiful view of the area, a yard that will easily fit an expansive garden, or a home with huge hallways perfect for wheelchair access. I also like to focus on sections of a community that I know are well positioned for private-pay clients. By that I mean individuals who pay out of pocket and are able to spend more than Medicaid/state-funded rates.

SETTING UP THE HOME IN THE RIGHT WAY

In my experience, getting the place is always the first step. Then it has to be made ready for the residential care business, and this usually includes remodels and meeting strict licensing requirements. Since I've worked on the construction side of this, I know very well what it is like to be involved in the building aspects. I love to envision a new space and then make it a reality.

During my years of running residential care homes, I've remodeled properties to make them a good fit and ensure they can be profitable. I've sat down and talked to countless contractors along the way about how senior-care home remodels are done. My goal has always been to make sure that all remodeled and constructed senior homes fit the needs of the elderly residents and attract high-paying clients. I know what works and what doesn't.

For instance, it's important to pay attention to the layout and flow of the home. I always analyze the floor plan to see where bathrooms are set up and how many more can be added. A residential care home with one main bathroom that four or five residents share will typically bring in less cash flow than a setup that has a private bath for each room. Take the position of a family touring a home for their aging relative. If they see a place that requires each senior to walk a long way to get to the bathroom and then are told their parent will share the tub that others use, they may be less interested (or will expect to pay a lower rate for the inconvenience). However, if they see that their loved one doesn't have to walk or be moved very far to get to the bathroom and can have private quarters, they may think that is a better arrangement—and be willing to pay for it. So for me, having more bathrooms often means higher cash flow.

Along those same lines, it's important that the home is easy to move through. I always make sure the hallways are wide and can fit a walker or wheelchair. I remove carpets and other features that could be potential hazards for seniors. Some considerations are things you might not think of right away but that really make a difference. For example, certain wall hangings could be upsetting to a senior with dementia or might be a safety concern. The elderly person could get scared or feel disturbed just by looking at an image. I know the kinds of pictures to avoid and which ones to put up. I have often selected quiet, serene displays of nature, like flowers or a tree or a lake landscape. These are typically calming and soothing for seniors to see. And I love a kitchen that is close to the living room or area where residents will often be, as it makes it easier for a caregiver to be cooking a meal and overseeing the residents at the same time.

There's a long list of details and requirements I go through during this step, which includes getting all the necessary approvals and licenses. This can vary from state to state, but think about why authorities establish these policies. Providers and caregivers will be taking on an ultra-important job, as they literally have the lives of seniors in their hands. State and local requirements are there to help ensure the home is as safe and well maintained as possible.

I've worked in the residential care home space for long enough to know that everything has to be done correctly right from the start. I also am keenly aware that once it's all in place, you have to monitor the codes and keep an eye out for changes. I have made adjustments over the years to meet the regulations in the areas where I have had homes and have a firm belief that everything—and I mean everything—has to be done by the letter of the law. It's simple: if you don't follow the rules, your home will be shut down. It's really a matter of the seniors' care and safety.

In my case, I tend to go above and beyond when it comes to getting everything right for the home, as I want to do all that I can to make the place a great one. The process always involves getting the right licensing approvals, meeting state and local codes, and installing all sorts of senior-friendly features like bathroom bars, well-lit living areas, and wheelchair ramps at the entrances. Then I take things even further to ensure an atmosphere where seniors truly thrive!

In addition to the remodeling process, whenever I've furnished residential care homes, I keep the seniors' best interests in mind. Suppose you and I are looking at a recliner to see if it would be a good fit. I will want one that is easy to sit on—and helps me to get up too. That's because elderly folks may need assistance as they ease into the chair and as they stand. The same is true for beds. I have always looked for features that help residents get in and out of their sleeping location easily and safely. Every piece of furniture has to be safe, comfortable, and senior-friendly.

In the previous chapter we talked about hiring staff and how complicated the process might be. When you work with me in a partnership, I'll provide guidance and help with these steps too. In my practice, I've spent years developing a hiring system that not only works but is also viewed as an outstanding process by caregivers and residents' families alike. To begin with, I've often found caregivers through the networks I've built up over my years of involvement in the senior-care and health industries. I've always been aware of what to include in my hiring practices to make sure everything is covered right from the start. This prevents discussions or conflicts that could come up later if everyone is not on the same page.

In addition, I've created a model that allows caregivers who meet certain job-related criteria to grow personally and advance in their careers. The system has consistently been a pretty big incentive for caregivers who want to do a good job and move up or even open their own residential care home in the future. It's like I say: you should give people room to improve and build themselves up, and then watch what they can do with the right motivation.

No residential care home can properly operate without the right supplies for its residents. Getting high-quality products while reducing overall spending is a specialty of mine. Here's why: this strategy provides top-notch products for seniors and also boosts the bottom line of the business, potentially leading to more returns for investors. For instance, I have always been a firm believer in fresh and nutritious food. When we make sure seniors have a diet that meets all their conditions and also their preferences, we can support their health and increase the chance that they will want to stay longer (rather than move to another care home).

Remember in Chapter 5, when we looked at the potential struggle to bring new residents into the home? You can be assured that I understand the marketing efforts needed and have plenty of experience filling homes. I'm also aware of which promotional efforts are worthwhile—and which ones aren't effective. During my years in the residential care business, I've held so many tours for families that I know exactly what to do. What I mean is that I can showcase a home and make family members who are visiting feel at ease as soon as they walk in. I know how to put up pictures and schedules where folks can easily see them. I understand how to lay out information on activities and excursions so people who are passing through stop and think, "Yes, I want to send my loved one here. This is the perfect place for them." But most importantly, I advise providers to keep every word and promise during this marketing effort. That's where the success begins! (Families remember the promises that are made on these tours, and sadly many facilities do not follow through.)

Based on my ability to run a home well, I've built up long waiting lists over the years. When I was involved as a provider, filling a spot for a home would often consist of looking at the waiting list and notifying the next family that a place was available for their loved one. In addition, it wasn't uncommon for the families of my residents to recommend my places to others who were looking for one. These word-of-mouth referrals made it easier to fill in vacancies when they arose. Much of this success could be attributed to my ability to keep my word and promises to families over the years.

Another important way that I can help as a partner, after the construction, remodeling, and licensing, is to identify ways to fill your home with residents. I can use my expertise to market the home and refer seniors to the right places. I draw on all my experiences in the residential care industry, including my deep knowledge and understanding of resident needs and family wishes. Along with these, I tap some of the established networks I've worked hard to build up over the years. Those that know me are aware of my strong desire to see the best experiences possible for the seniors, their families, caregivers, providers, and investors. When everything comes together and an elderly person finds the perfect home, it is so rewarding to observe this complex system in action and the happy environment as an outcome.

As with other points, if you have experience in marketing, you're welcome to do part of this process on your own. You also could partner with someone else. If you do, use the examples I've given to help guide your efforts. And remember that by contacting me, we can set up a customized arrangement that best suits your specific needs. Whatever route you choose, the long-term goal should always be to take care of the senior first and foremost, and the business results will inevitably follow.

RUNNING A RESIDENTIAL CARE HOME WITH A PARTNER

If you thought your role when working with me—which we could call "the Nelly Way"—would be easy, just wait till I explain this step to you. Don't worry, it's good news: your job is about to get even easier. No need to check on the place every day, see how the caregivers are doing, talk to the family members, and count how many supplies are on hand. While all these things might be enjoyable—and I'm not saying they're dreary— what I'm getting at is that they are also very time-consuming.

Instead, a partnership with me allows you to have a passive investment. You won't have to carry out the daily logistics or make calls every week. I know how to make arrangements and ensure that the business is set up to be successful. I will connect you with the provider and train them so they can run the home well and employ great caregivers. (If you're a provider or caregiver, contact me as well! I wrote this book for you too and am always open to talking about possibilities.) I will coach the provider through all the steps so that they have and maintain all the licenses. But most importantly, I will show them how to run a profitable business with seniors who are thriving.

This strategy provides benefits for both the investor and the provider.

If you're an investor, you can have peace of mind that the provider, who will be your property's tenant, is well trained to run the business. As a landlord/investor, you'll be well positioned to receive a high cash flow and have a steady client on the rental property. For providers, you'll have access to my business training and high standards and can apply my guidance to the home.

Throughout it all, I will coordinate these arrangements and prioritize high-quality care, safety, and fulfillment for seniors. For example, I always explain to providers how demanding but also rewarding this business can be. I help them understand that a senior could have an emergency at any time and need to be taken in for treatment. To really provide holistic care, they'll have a system in place that allows for someone on staff to go with the senior whenever they travel to an outside medical facility, especially in an emergency. There the care worker can assist in explaining the elderly individual's condition (especially if they suffer from dementia) and serve as a health advocate.

This is just one of the many instances I provide coaching on as I make sure providers are well equipped to handle the important task of caring for seniors. For this reason, when you work with me in a partnership, you can have the comfort of knowing that I'm keeping seniors and their well-being as our number one goal. When this happens and elderly individuals thrive, business tends to perform better. The tenants are satisfied, the investors receive their return, and everyone involved gets the chance to help improve the daily lives of the aging population.

If by chance you decide you want to carry out this investment and arrangement on your own, you can still reach out to me, and I'll coach you on how best to get started. Perhaps you have a home you don't live in that you want to turn into a residential care home. Or you love remodeling and have worked in the renovation space for several decades. You might not, however, have any experience turning residential homes into places where seniors live. In a case such as this one, you may be eager to help out with certain aspects when setting up the property. When you and I talk, we can write out an agreement that works well for you. I'll provide assistance in the areas where you might not have experience or that you don't feel comfortable handling.

I bring this up to show you that if you want to be more involved, your arrangements will look different from the option of taking a hands-off approach. There isn't a right or wrong method here (except, of course, if you go with a partner who doesn't know what they are doing, in which case, watch out!). The idea is that a partnership agreement will accommodate your goals and skills. I'm happy to meet you where you are and work with you so you can participate as much, or as little, as you'd like in the residential care home investment.

Regardless of your situation, it's not out of the ordinary to expect, as an investor, that you'll get more cash flow if you work with me as your partner versus adopting the DIY method. Keep in mind if you take the DIY approach, it can be difficult to scale, as some states may only allow you to be a provider in one home or have other restrictions. However, if you are an investor, it can be easier to scale up and have two, three, or more investments. To do so, it makes sense to have a partner. It's extremely helpful if the partner—i.e., "Nelly"—has ample experience and knows the best practices you'll need to follow to make the business lucrative (which we'll cover more thoroughly in the next chapter). A healthy business partnership will increase the chances of your investment's success.

LET'S WORK TOGETHER

Finally, I think it's essential in this space to find a partner who can really make a home shine. I've done this in the past, time and again. And I've seen how a happy, healthy environment is so different, sadly, from many other places. Family members pay attention too.

Consider this following true example from a case study backed by the National Institute of Nursing Research that interviewed individuals about finding care for their older loved ones. Carolyn,[66] the daughter of an eighty-year-old man with Parkinson's disease, felt discouraged after looking for a home that would fit her father's needs. "You can see all kinds of houses out there, and a lot of them were . . . you know, I wouldn't want to put my parent into one of them," she said.[67] After discussing all this, it's clear that it takes an exceptionally run home to grab the attention of family members and convince them that they should place their loved one there. It also requires ongoing attention to detail and communication to make the arrangement continue to work.

As we've seen in these last chapters, the key to success lies in doing good for others and focusing on high-quality care for seniors. That's why it's even more important to partner with me, because my passion for seniors drives my business. We'll look at top strategies for making a place stand out among the competition in the next chapter.

As you read on, keep in mind that these practices are really my secret sauce: it is a system I developed based on my experience in the senior-care industry and my desire to help this group of individuals. It's how I show love to the elderly while also helping others who want to be involved in the senior-care industry. It's a setup that allows investors to partner with me, ultimately bringing more gains for everyone. Luckily for you, I'm sharing these best practices here so you can learn from my design and be ready to shake hands with me so we can get to work making good—and even great—things happen. Together, we can work as like-minded individuals who share a commitment to affect the lives of seniors, allowing them to truly thrive—and also succeed in every aspect of the business.

CHAPTER 7

Best Practices for High Cash Flow

I spent the last two chapters laying out the basics for getting started with a residential care home. The approaches—DIY and with a partner—differ greatly, but they do share a common goal. That's to create a space for seniors where they can receive the care they need and live in an environment that's clean and functional and that encourages them to thrive. The arrangement also aims to keep their families satisfied and provide easy channels of open communication for everyone.

It would be simplistic to assume that the scenario ends here. Behind every great business plan is a set of nuts and bolts that really holds everything together. The logistical details keep operations running smoothly *and* turning a considerable profit. Think of it as if you're attending a beautiful opera at a high-end theater: the singing is outstanding, the music sounds divine, and the meal served during intermission tastes superb. It all seems so effortless, but if you went backstage, you'd find the true reason you enjoyed the concert. There's a system in place that may look a bit chaotic at times but is designed to make the front stage function in a way that enables the audience to love what they hear, see, and taste and inspires them to come back again and again.

Note the last part of that sentence: the audience returns to repeat the activity. Assuming the manager is putting best practices into place, this cycle ensures that a chunk of change is being made during every performance. The people running the show have developed a system that looks beautiful on the outside, draws a faithful following, and brings in plenty of profit.

Now, let's shift our focus back to our topic of residential care. The home needs to look and feel fabulous—*and* it has to make money every month. It should go without saying that to truly be successful, there needs to be significantly more money coming in than going out to cover all the money already spent on setting up and starting the business.

I'll be honest—there are certain things that just come naturally for me. Over the years, I built up my business by knowing deep in my heart that the top priority was to take good care of people and go the extra mile. I have always been firmly committed to giving seniors the respect and treatment they deserve. By doing that, I intuitively felt the rewards would come. And they have, time and again.

Throughout the process of designing my business model, I didn't use a how-to guide that laid out, step-by-step, how to turn a profit. I simply followed my heart and passion as guiding lights when caring for people. I made decisions based on what I felt would be best for everyone.

In addition, while building my own business model, I drew from my experiences in the healthcare establishments where I had worked in the past. I clearly recalled events I had seen and never wanted to repeat. As a result, the system that I use today was created organically. I adjusted the model over time to hone best practices in the care industry.

As with many things in life, others noticed how well my residential care homes were doing and asked me to share the secrets of my success. To answer their questions, I had to take a step back and think about the system I had established. After looking around and comparing my homes to others, I realized that my places indeed stood out in several ways, including bringing in a cash flow that was much higher than the average for the residential care home segment.

In this chapter, I'll lay out the areas to focus on in order to generate a high cash flow in this field. Before doing so, however, I want to highlight the point that by putting the following guidelines in place, you (or you and your partner working together) will be able to create the ideal environment. Let's look at some of the risks involved in this industry first. We'll then study how much of a difference high-quality care and best practices can make.

PROBLEMS WITH ELDER ABUSE

Whenever we talk about the residential care home as an industry, we need to keep in mind that we're dealing with people's lives. Homes that single-mindedly focus on cost-cutting measures will ultimately fail. Sadly, some places have closed their doors, but in my opinion, it would have been far worse to force residents into subpar and even inhumane living conditions.

Throughout the senior care segment, abuse has always been a cause of great concern. One resident in a nursing home in Georgia saw elder neglect in action. "My roommate—they throw him in the bed," the resident stated. "They handle him any kind of way. He can't take up for himself."[68] In another case in Texas, a family member shared what she observed when her mother spent time living in a nursing home. "Have I seen abuse?" the daughter said. "No, not directly. But I've come in and found my mom battered and bruised. I mean, her whole face was bruised and swollen, the backs of her hands and arms were bruised, as if she tried to protect herself."[69] And a caregiver in South Carolina described what can go on within a senior home: "Oh yeah, I've seen abuse. Things like rough handling, pinching, pulling too hard on a resident to make them do what you want. Slapping, that too. People get so tired—working mandatory overtime, being short-staffed. It's not an excuse, but it makes it so hard for them to respond right."[70]

Since abuse remains an issue in the senior care industry, adult children are highly aware of the risks they're taking when they place their aged relative in a home. They may ask questions to explore the possibilities of neglect or abuse. And while regulations have certainly helped alleviate many abuse-related risks, families need assurance. They have to feel comfortable about leaving their loved one in a residential care home. If they drop off their mother or father and then spend sleepless nights worrying about what's going on in the home, they'll likely move the resident to a different one in the near future.

Given this, it takes a pretty great setup to convince adult children that they should leave a parent or grandparent in the home. If that's not what they find—if, for example, they see old food left out on the kitchen table or smell an off odor in the living room—they will turn away and look for a better location for their loved one.

Sometimes, residential care homes become a place where elderly folks can really suffer. Several years ago, cases of rampant neglect of residents were reported in Seattle, and some homes had to shut down as a result.[71] The good news is that these situations can be avoided if you follow my advice for best practices.

These methods may seem counterintuitive when it comes to producing a high cash flow, but I have discovered, through my own experiences, that spending more in certain areas can often lead to higher levels of income later. This contradicts age-old business ideas that encourage cutting expenses by doing things like hiring cheap labor, buying generic products that sacrifice quality for low prices, and avoiding maintenance measures to reduce property costs. I haven't followed any of those strategies and find most of them appalling.

Instead, my set of best practices for a high cash flow focuses on quality care, along with putting an ongoing branding strategy into place. These guidelines also cover creating a positive, encouraging environment for seniors with activity options such as outings, gardening opportunities, and the chance to participate in their favorite pastimes. My final best practice encompasses the ever-important tool of communication to build relationships. Creating an open environment, listening to residents and families, and being ready to converse with them in an honest, efficient way is vital.

Let's get started.

BEST PRACTICE #1: PROVIDING A HIGH LEVEL OF CARE

When I have welcomed a new resident into one of my homes, I have always asked extensive questions to get to know the person: What did they like to do when they lived on their own? What did they like to eat? When would they have their breakfast in the morning? When the resident or their family answered these questions, I would listen carefully while taking extensive notes.

The responses would tell me a lot. I could understand if their loved one was the type of person who was always looking for a lot of things to do, or if they never really enjoyed exercise. I could see if they preferred to be around people, or if their social calendar was pretty free and they enjoyed their alone time. I might hear about their love of classical concerts or knitting. I could be told that they never played cards before and didn't care to participate in group games.

In addition to interests, I would learn about their health history and the assessments that their doctors and medical team created for them. This would allow me to determine what kind of care they would need in our home. They might have memory problems, like the onset of dementia, or mobility challenges and other age-related disabilities that might need closer attention.

All this information is invaluable. I would use the answers I received from asking these questions to set up a tailored care plan. If the family told me their father always had a big breakfast at about 10:30 a.m., there's no reason he would have to be served every day at 8:00 a.m. unless he chose to! Even if the other residents liked to dine earlier, we could make arrangements for a caregiver to provide his meal at the time he preferred in the morning.

Let me pause quickly here. You might be reading through this and thinking, "Aren't we talking about best practices for running a business? Shouldn't we be streamlining everything?" It's true that it might take longer for a caregiver to serve residents at different times. But that's all taken into account in the business plan. I've always made sure caregivers aren't too strapped—it's not good to have them feeling frazzled and leaving residents to wait for an hour or longer while they are busy tending to everyone else. You'll remember that this is the exact problem I mentioned when it comes to much larger senior facilities, like nursing homes and assisted-living centers. The number of residents living in these places is frequently just too high to have caregivers accommodate everyone's preferences. These operations are certainly run on a more streamlined basis. Meals must be mass-produced for everyone, a schedule needs to be followed to ensure each resident is served a meal, and so on. Recall that in these large facilities, caregivers are frequently given so many residents to care for that they can't possibly carve out personal time for individual residents. Consider how much more a caregiver who is tending to two seniors can do for those individuals than a caregiver who is running around trying to help eighteen seniors with their everyday activities. A caregiver overseeing a couple of elderly people can give each of them breakfast whenever they want it. The caregiver can also stop and ask them if they liked the meal. How were the eggs? Do they want them cooked the same way next time? Do they want a different meal tomorrow? In other words, there is time to have a real conversation and form a relationship, which is something nearly all seniors truly crave and value (and is often hard to find in other facilities).

When I set up a care plan, I have always accounted for the specific nutritional needs of the resident. Now, most seniors have general dietary requirements that help them to feel and function at their best. For instance, drinking lots of water (which I admit that not everyone likes to do) is important for good digestion. There may be some more specific needs for an individual too, based on their health conditions. Maybe they are allergic to dairy or nuts. With a detailed list of any specific requirements, it is easier to work those into meal plans.

Food and nutrition play a big role in providing a high level of care for residents. This is logical: take a moment and think about how much better you feel if you eat at regular times, consume plenty of fruits and vegetables, and make sure you're hydrated. And you probably function better during the week if you eat healthy meals at home compared to a series of meals grabbed at irregular times from fast-food restaurants. When it comes to seniors, this nutrition game is even more vital. By this, I mean that the food a senior eats on a regular basis has an even greater impact on their overall well-being than what a teenager eats. A younger person's entire body system is in a different, stronger stage, and the effects may not be seen or felt right away. Serve a senior a series of highly processed meals, however, and they will not feel as good as if they had eaten organic, vegetable-heavy dishes.

For this reason, I have always made sure that nutritious meals are provided continually. One of my biggest rules has been no canned food. Everything should be made from scratch. Since most residents who have lived in my homes need a diet that is full of vegetables and water to help with digestion, we have always served plenty of fresh soups. We also bake whole-grain bread, blend up lots of smoothies, and use very little salt in our dishes.

I've always been careful to keep sugar to a minimum in every meal plan. I wouldn't necessarily cut it off entirely, though. As I mentioned earlier, part of my approach to treating seniors well includes understanding the things they love and are an important part of their regular routine. For many people, sweets can be a source of joy. We would typically serve a dessert twice to three times a week to seniors whose medical conditions allowed them to indulge. This would give them something to look forward to as well. For instance, they might have known they wouldn't eat dessert on Wednesdays, but every Saturday they could expect ice cream after dinner.

Besides food, a high level of care encompasses the residents' overall sense of cleanliness and hygiene. This arrangement caters to each resident's needs, and I have set it up in all my homes. I follow the care plan strictly and look for ways to do more than what is required. My homes stand out because I always make sure I have enough highly trained staff on hand to tend to the seniors' care details around the clock. Having caregivers who can provide one-on-one attention reduces the risk of skin issues that can result from poor hygiene routines. This system ensures that seniors are well taken care of and maintain their sense of dignity.

As we can see, top-notch caregivers really make a difference. They are the people who interact with the residents on a continual basis. If a caregiver gets to know each resident individually and thinks of them like a family member, they will be more inclined to listen to the resident's individual needs and requests. The caregiver will also be more likely to take action based on what they hear. I'll cover this point more in the next chapter.

Perhaps Tom, the new gentleman who arrived a couple of weeks ago, says that he prefers his coffee to be served before breakfast, rather than with the meal. "Very well," a caring caregiver responds. The next day, the caregiver delivers a fresh, steaming mug of coffee before breakfast, much to Tom's delight.

In my homes, I've never had a resident move out because they or their family were unhappy with the quality of care they received. In the industry of senior care, this is a true indicator of the level of service that my homes provide. Residents are satisfied with their meals and happy with their caregivers, and they feel like they are part of a family.

By paying attention to the details I listed above, you can expect to have a lower turnover rate, which means fewer breaks in the cash flow for a home. In other words, well-cared-for residents stay. And when they do, consistent monthly payments follow.

BEST PRACTICE #2: PICK YOUR BRANDING—AND STICK TO IT

Let's start this section with a fun story. I have typically had a little garden in the backyard of each of my homes, which produces lovely fresh vegetables like tomatoes and lettuce. We would use our produce in lots of dishes, fulfilling those nutritional needs I mentioned before.

Interestingly, our gardens have served another purpose, one that would often be pure joy to watch. Whenever a new resident would enter one of my homes, I would let them know they were welcome to spend time in the garden. While our caregivers, staff, and I would oversee the logistics of the vegetable patch, making sure everything was planted correctly, watered, and weeded, the residents could come out to the garden and simply enjoy the space.

Here's how the scene would often play out. Say an elderly woman named Nettie moved into the residential care home during the spring. Her family shared with us that she used to have a garden at her former home. In fact, planting and harvesting were annual rituals she used to carry out in her own yard. "That's wonderful," I would say after they described her love for gardening. "Did you know we have a garden in the backyard? She can come out whenever she wants to spend time there."

Nettie would get settled into her new home, our residential care home. After a couple of weeks, she would have a morning routine pretty well established. She would take her breakfast at 9:00 a.m. and then spend a little time in a chair overlooking the backyard. After that, she would go out to the garden for a little bit. She might feel like being more active, so she would pull a few weeds. Or she might just want to look at the progress of the various vegetable plants.

The goal wasn't to have Nettie follow a gardening routine or put hours of labor into the planting and harvesting. Rather, the aim was always to give her that feeling of independence she associated with gardening. Spending time in this green space could also help her remember the things she used to love doing there. She might share some of her tips and stories with a caregiver, who would listen to every word and agree with her that it was a special activity. The garden then would become a place that allowed residents to create—on a smaller scale—a hobby from the past that was prominent in their lives at one point.

I have always loved giving my residents an opportunity to engage in activities that have been meaningful to them. But by this point, you may be wondering what gardening has to do with branding, a best practice I mentioned earlier. In fact, it has a lot to do with it. Let me explain why.

If you took a tour of one of the properties I've overseen, you would note one factor in common: they are expansive. I come from the countryside and am used to big spaces and green scenery. I personally love the feeling of being in nature, of having that opportunity to sit out on the porch and look at an ample backyard. I revel in the chance to walk along a path surrounded by trees and flowering bushes while taking in the fresh air. For this reason, I have tended to purchase properties for my residential care homes that are close to an acre in size. While this may not be large by rural standards, it is a fairly substantial plot of land for a residential area in a suburb, which is where I have typically placed homes.

After securing property of an acre or so, I would have more flowers and trees planted, in addition to putting the aforementioned vegetable garden in place. When I was through, the finished area would be colorful, full of life, and arrayed with flowerpots. Furthermore, the property would always be meticulously maintained. The nature aspect is one of the first things visitors and families notice.

If you spend some time touring other residential care homes, you'll find that expansive, immaculate grounds aren't to be found at every place. And I'm not saying each home must have a large property; the point I'm making is that you have to pick your branding and think about what sets you apart. For me, the initial branding has definitely been all about a beautiful, big yard and well-kept garden. For others, it might be a smaller property with a bigger-than-average vegetable garden. Or perhaps it's a small yard with no garden that has a large outdoor patio where residents can sit for hours to enjoy the outdoors.

Creating a brand goes beyond the outside, of course. After visitors take in a first impression of your exterior, they'll be interested in seeing what's inside. And what they find there is equally important. I have focused on practical, comfortable furniture within the home. Everything has been kept clutter-free, as this helps prevent falls and accidents. I have kept enough decorations on the walls and accents throughout the place to give the space a homelike atmosphere.

When people tour my spaces, they notice that everyone on the staff (usually including me) is dressed the same. I require all my employees to wear a hunter-green uniform with white socks and white tennis shoes. If the weather is cool, a long-sleeved white shirt can be worn underneath the outfit.

Collectively, this all—the garden, the large property, the homey, well-kept interiors, and a professional staff—has worked together to form my brand. It's important that residents and their families can easily see what the home is like, understand how we operate, and associate themes like cleanliness and space with my residences. Again, like my other practices, I have built up a brand based on my genuine concern for the elderly along with my past experiences in senior care.

To fully comprehend the importance of a solid brand, think about the flip side. If you have an average-looking home on an average-looking property filled with average-attired caregivers, what will your residents expect? Moreover, what rate can you list for a monthly rent? Certainly not a higher-than-average amount. Who would be willing to pay more for something that looks on the outside, as well as on the inside, nothing but average?

Your brand will help establish the rate you can ask residents to pay. If you aim for an average brand, you can likely charge an average rate. You'll then make sure the money coming in covers your expenses. I have found, however, that this type of setting is almost never one that can lead to a high cash flow. That's because by keeping the rate at an average level—or below average—you'll naturally start searching for ways to lower the costs necessary to run the place. And that can lead to a drop in the level of care or the quality of the home, which can quickly be catastrophic for the business.

On the other hand, I have found that a higher rate can be charged by building a brand that focuses on quality care and is appealing to the eye, an especially important aspect to catch the attention of the families of potential residents. This higher rate can then cover the needed expenses and bring in plenty of funds without having to cut corners anywhere. It's a bit like this: build it big and beautiful, and residents (and their families) will expect to pay more for the top-notch care and quality.

Once you have a brand in place, you'll want to avoid the danger of flip-flopping around. A family who visits your place one year and finds it in great shape and then returns a year later to see that it has been run down will not be pleased. In fact, they may be likely to share their negative opinion with others, who will listen. All this could eventually hurt your brand, the number of residents you have, and the cash flow you bring in.

I have built up my brand in a certain way and worked year after year to maintain consistency. This has given residents the benefit of knowing what to expect. As word of mouth spread, which is the way most of my homes have been filled, individuals could assure others that my places remained the same in the best possible ways.

The cornerstone of the brand is putting the residents first. When this happens, families always take note and often comment on it. This feature stands out compared to other places that don't prioritize well-being.

The cash flow incentive here is that you have low turnover. In a residential care home, filled beds equate to a consistent cash flow. Likewise, a high-quality brand provides the chance to charge a rate that aligns with the amenities offered in the home.

BEST PRACTICE #3: A POSITIVE ENVIRONMENT FOR ACTIVITIES

Do you think promoting something like "We Play Bingo" will draw in more residents? Will it allow you to charge a higher rate? Will you be able to bring in more cash, given that your place offers an additional amenity?

If you are shaking your head no, congratulations. You are starting to grasp my emphasis on targeting the individual need, rather than showcasing generic, group-minded features that may (or may not) appeal to the masses. I bring this up as a bit of a joke, but the truth is clear. I have had families come into my homes and ask about their parent playing bingo. *They* think it would be a great way for Mom to spend her time. "I don't see anything wrong with that," you may be thinking. It is nice that they want to keep her happy, well cared for, and active, but the problem occurs when it turns out Mom doesn't want to play bingo. For instance, pretend she comes into one of the homes I have overseen, and I automatically agree with the family to make sure she attends a bingo session every Tuesday night. I don't ask the mom if she wants to participate in these weekly games. What do you think will happen next? I've seen it play out in several ways. Maybe Mom will refuse to go to bingo night and the family then wonders why Mom isn't getting in enough activities and socializing. Or maybe Mom will attend bingo night a few times and then stop going, and again, the family asks me, "Why isn't she spending time with other seniors?" A third possibility could also develop. Mom goes to bingo night regularly, and the family believes all is well, but all is not well. Mom is miserable. And maybe she complains about it, or maybe she faithfully goes week after week and just puts up with an activity she hates because she doesn't think she has a choice. Either way, the situation is not good for her. And as I've emphasized continually, neglecting to find out what residents *really* want and not striving to help them do the things they *really* love is a recipe for poor well-being. One way or another, the situation will deteriorate.

"OK," you may be thinking, "what do seniors really want?" Sit down and ask six seniors what they want, and you'll likely get six different responses. Elderly people are just as unique and varied as younger people. There's a certain beauty in this individualism, but establishing a routine that accommodates a person's preferences is a bit of an art.

Here's why: Elderly individuals will indeed have opinions about what they want to do and what they don't want to do. So will their families. And then there's the third factor you have to account for—the senior's health. Think of a scenario where Mom crocheted for several decades. She loved to make doilies and often gifted her creations to others. Naturally, when her daughter and son-in-law start looking for a residential care home for her, they keep this in mind. Say their mother has moved into one of my homes and the children come up to me and say they'd like a caregiver to spend time twice a week with Mom so she can continue crocheting. The daughter and son-in-law look at each other and smile knowingly. They are hoping to help Mom continue a pastime they know she has long enjoyed.

I would be all for Mom continuing to do what she loves. What happens, though, if Mom can no longer see well enough to properly use a hook and yarn? Now take it a step further: If I don't investigate this beforehand, what happens when a caregiver pulls out the hooks, needles, and yarn for her? In ten minutes, maybe Mom has unfortunately poked herself in the eye. Now we have an injured senior, a caregiver in a frenzy to help, other residents thrown off their schedules, and a daughter and son-in-law who are upset that Mom is injured and not able to do what she loves anymore.

This is an unfortunate situation. It is also one that I have avoided in my homes. The conversation that the daughter and son-in-law began about wanting Mom to crochet? With me, no final decisions would have been made without going over a few questions to first gain some insight. After listening to their request that a caregiver help Mom with her crocheting hobby, I would ask, "Does she still crochet?" If the daughter responded that Mom doesn't crochet anymore, I might ask why. I would also explore with Mom if she were actually interested in crocheting. If I learned she still wants to crochet but doesn't see well, I would continue to explore the possibilities. Just because she has poor eyesight doesn't mean she can no longer do anything crochet-related. It simply means we may need to be extra creative. I might work with a caregiver, for instance, to help Mom hold the yarn and a crocheted item. In this case, she doesn't actually do any crocheting, but she can look at the pretty colors and handiwork and remember how she liked to crochet in the past. (This activity may seem bland, but for residents with common neurodegenerative illnesses such as Alzheimer's, it can actually be very satisfying.)

Here's where I'm going with this—creating a positive, upbeat environment for seniors that includes activities they love is a great best practice. In my homes, we have specialized in making these activities come to life. They don't have to be regular (like the gardening I discussed, seniors can do it whenever they want) or strenuous, but they do need to fulfill a role.

In the scenario about crocheting, note that Mom didn't actually spend time making gifts or doilies anymore. Holding a crocheted object in her hand and being near the tools used to make it served as a way to think about her life and enjoy the moment.

As another example, let's consider a resident who loves the piano. Say his name is Joseph, and he used to play for public engagements as a side job but also had a piano in his home and filled the space with music for years. Now he would love to continue playing. Let's pretend he has learned that one of my residential care homes has a well-maintained upright piano. "Perfect," the family might think. I, however, would first ask Joseph if he still wants to play. He might tell me he can't anymore because his fingers hurt too much from arthritis. He learned while living in his home that if he played for thirty minutes in the morning, he might have to spend the entire afternoon resting his hands as much as possible because his fingers ached so badly from the activity. I would then talk to the family and lay out some options. Maybe if Joseph wants to keep playing, we could seek a doctor's opinion about ways to help with the pain in his fingers. Or we could talk to Joseph about what music he likes to play and then play it on the radio or stereo for him at a certain time each day. In that case, other residents might sit with him and listen to the jazz he loves. By talking through his options and setting up a plan, we could find a solution for helping Joseph do what he wants or to relive his hobby in a certain way.

Nothing is permanent, of course. Maybe we took Joseph to the doctor and he received some medicine that really helped and allowed him to play in the mornings for a little bit. After a few months, he might tell me his fingers don't hurt anymore, but he'd prefer to just listen to the tunes rather than play. "No problem," I would say. We would also discuss it with his family so they would know we were making a change and that it was with Joseph's preferences and best interests in mind.

You might be thinking by now that these families are sometimes unaware, wondering, "How can they not know what their loved one is capable of doing?" The truth is their aging relative might hide how they feel. They might put on a good face when visiting with family so no one worries about them but then suffer the aftermath when visiting time is over. If a parent always read books in the past and there is a stack of books out on the table when the family comes over, it might be easy to assume the parent is still reading. Maybe their eyesight is too poor, however, and they are merely bringing out their favorite works to remember what it was like to turn the page.

I don't bring up these examples to imply negligence. In fact, most families who come to me deeply love their aging relative. They are very concerned and want this stage of their loved one's life to be the best it can be. And I have always supported that desire. What we often don't realize, however, is that the elderly individual is changing. This shift is a big one that affects both that person and their families. In many senses, the senior is losing that precious sense of independence they had for so long. While families are extremely concerned, they might not know the best questions to ask or how to handle the situation exactly.

That's where my business model comes in. I have been exposed to so many different senior situations that I've set guidelines to help providers and caregivers make those specific and useful inquiries, delve deep to find the root of a problem, and then solve it for everyone. I know that if everyone involved works to get to the bottom of an issue, they can then all rise to the top together. This, in turn, leads to happy residents and content families.

Take, for instance, the following case. The adult children of an aging woman came looking for a place for their mom to live and said to me, "She has burns all over herself and we don't know why." They were really worried and added, "She has dementia and might be doing something she shouldn't be."

I didn't berate the grown children for not looking into the matter more vigorously, and I certainly didn't accuse their mother of anything. Instead, I posed some questions to gain a fuller picture. "Does she smoke?" I asked. It turned out that the mother had been a heavy smoker all her life. Then I suggested a possible scenario of what was happening based on what I had seen other seniors do during my time in the healthcare industry. "Your mom, whom I know you love deeply, may be smoking on her own," I said.

The adult children responded that they suspected the same thing, even though they knew she shouldn't be smoking on her own anymore. She apparently found it very hard to quit. I suggested one option I had witnessed in similar settings, which involved working with a medical team. A doctor might be able to prescribe something that could help their mother overcome the withdrawal that would happen from giving up cigarettes. Another option I presented included having a caregiver sit with her while she simply held a pipe or an unlit cigarette to remember the act and still break away from it. If the home had a designated outdoor smoking area, we could discuss that possibility too.

By laying out a path for the future together, I explained to her family, we could resolve two issues. First, we could help their mother avoid getting more burns, and second, we could help her stop smoking. We could do it in a fashion that was humane and accounted for her potential withdrawal symptoms.

At the heart of any activity offered to a senior should be an aspect of independence. By making an elderly person feel that they are still able to function, participate, and be productive, they can maintain a sense of purpose. This doesn't mean the senior has to be completely independent and cook dinner on their own; rather, it's about creating an atmosphere that allows them to contribute in their own way.

It is very difficult for a senior to give up their autonomy, and it is often hard for a family to witness and be a part of this transition as well. In a way, they have to admit their parent is shifting into another stage of life, and it's not uncommon to find a grown child who is simply in denial. It's hard to watch someone lose the ability to carry out a pastime they loved for years on end and was very much a part of who they were as an individual, let alone see them slowly lose their identity through progressive dementia.

This best practice of working collaboratively really shines through in the homes I have developed when consideration is given to discover what the family wants and what the resident wants. Then we can figure out what is possible. We put our heads together as a unit and develop a plan that is practical and pleasing. My homes have become places where residents really thrive, and their families marvel at the environment we've created for them.

It's not uncommon for a family to take a tour of a home that follows my business model and find a resident helping in the kitchen. Many of the residents enjoyed cooking and preparing meals in their earlier lives. They may no longer be able to bake a pie on their own or use the stovetop to cook, but they can certainly help caregivers. You might find an elderly resident washing the lettuce that was just picked from the garden and will be used in a salad for dinner. Another resident may be stirring flour and other dry ingredients together in a bowl to help a staff member bake bread.

While I love to focus on individuals, the activities I have provided in my homes also include some group options. One regular activity I've had in place for years in my residential care home plan that has continually received positive feedback is the group outing. Staff might take residents to a restaurant once or twice a month, to a park, or to visit a local event. Team members snap pictures during the field trips and print some of them to put up on a bulletin board for everyone to see.

This serves so many wonderful purposes. It helps families understand what their loved one is doing and see a real record of the good times they are having. The outings also allow residents to get out of the home and have a sense of independence and feel like they are participating in something they can do on their own (or with some help).

You may be asking, "How does this best practice lead to high cash flow?" By focusing on holistically integrating activities into the daily lives of residents, you'll create happier individuals who are more likely to stay, and their families will see that you are genuinely looking out for their loved ones. You are also building a brand that allows for charging higher rates, which, as noted earlier, can lead to better cash flow all around.

BEST PRACTICE #4: MONITORING MULTIFACETED RELATIONSHIPS

In hard financial terms, turnover is what can kill a residential care business. Empty beds mean no monthly rent payment, while filled beds mean residents who are paying (or have family members who are paying). Demonstrating to families that you are committed to their loved ones really helps them see that you take the business—and their parent—seriously. That's why building strong relationships is a solid best practice I have long put into effect. Forming solid bonds with families has, in turn, led to filled beds and solid monetary results.

Under my business model, when a new family is brought in, it's important for providers and caregivers to really get to know them. Team members engage in a way that addresses the concerns the family has about their loved one being admitted to a care facility. To do this, it's important to ask questions to understand the level of assistance needed and to address issues related to medicines and activities.

But there's more to it than that. During these initial conversations, the families are being screened. They undergo a process to help providers and caregivers determine if their loved one should be admitted to the place. There are two red flags to look for: extreme health conditions and family drama.

Regarding health, if the resident needs a higher level of care than can be provided, it's important to recommend the family go somewhere else. For instance, perhaps the resident is currently in the hospital and really needs to stay there. The provider can share that opinion with the family. Doing what's best for the individual is what's most important and overrides the need to keep beds filled.

Having to turn away a resident because they need more care is a rare occurrence, though. Because the home plan I've developed provides around-the-clock caregivers who can focus on individual needs, it's possible to accommodate most residents, regardless of their health. Specialists, therapists, and other healthcare professionals also help with this and come to the home to treat the residents and work with them regularly. I simply mention it here because, during the screening process, it's essential to make sure the resident will receive the best care possible. If the level of assistance they need is only available somewhere else, they should be aware of their options.

Now, let's tackle family drama. Oh yes, everyone has it. I'll be the first to admit that my family is not immune. I am quick to empathize with other families going through tense situations, which often occur when a family is transferring a loved one from their own home to a supervised residence. However, drama has its limits.

Through my business model, when a family is screened, it's vital to be on the lookout for signs of extreme conflict. It's simply not a good idea to allow a family's fighting to affect the well-being of the other residents. One big indicator of trouble often arises with the power of attorney, which is a document allowing someone else to make decisions on your behalf. For residents in a care facility, a power of attorney is common. However, if the family has two powers of attorney, or no designated power of attorney, a storm could be brewing. That's because the provider and caregivers will need to work with multiple family members to make decisions for their loved one. What happens if there are two powers of attorney and they don't see eye to eye? Or if they make polar-opposite decisions? Along the same lines, there can be issues if there is no power of attorney in place, as it will be difficult to find someone to make choices for the senior.

In such cases, it's often useful to pull the family members aside and carefully explain that having no power of attorney, or more than one power of attorney, can lead to sticky disputes. This can help reduce later conflicts. The family might decide to establish a power of attorney if they don't have one in place. If they have two, we may discuss who will be the main contact for the senior in our home and also set ground rules prior to admission to avoid family disputes at the senior home.

At the end of the day, the screening is done because it's critical to have a family who is ready to work with a provider and caregivers, participate in their senior's well-being, and get along with everyone else during the process. And trust me, this doesn't always happen spontaneously and automatically. In my homes, if I saw a family of a senior come in for a tour and noticed a huge conflict surfacing among them, I would say something. I might even suggest they need to address their differences among themselves for the benefit of their loved one's care. I've never tried to be rude; I've simply looked out for the best interests of everyone.

Now, I know we've talked about how difficult it can be to bring in residents and maintain filled beds. Being picky about who is allowed in might seem to work against that point. Shouldn't we just jump at any family and any paying resident we can find?

I'll be the first to say that bringing in a medical condition you can't support or allowing drama from one family to leak into the lives of others will ultimately lead to a poor cash flow. You'll spend so much time focusing on one resident and their family that it will be detrimental to others. It's also emotionally draining for the provider and caregivers to be stuck in the middle of disputes. Given this, if you allow in family issues, you could lose other residents. You could also hurt your reputation and brand. Both will result in a loss of income, and it could even be difficult to bring in new residents after word of mouth has spread.

Once residents are settled into a home, it's necessary for them to stay very connected to their families and establish clear channels of communication with them. If a provider or caregiver thinks a change should be made to the resident's care plan, they will need to let the family members know. In my homes, I have often served as a go-between for different parts of the resident's care: I would talk to the families, the residents, the caregivers, the various individuals coming in to provide services . . . in short, everyone. And I loved this aspect. You really have to if you're going to run a successful residential care home and make it a place that brings in high cash flow.

I've laid out four best practices, which include the level of care, branding, activities, and relationships. As you incorporate these, you'll want to make sure you keep the big picture in mind. By that, I mean you have to keep your overall expenses within the limits you have set. If you plan to charge residents $5,000 a month and have six residents, obviously purchasing a $12 million property will not match up.

That said, these best practices are only part of the pie when building a successful residential care home. To fully complete it, you need a culture that encourages residents to thrive and shows them that you care.

It's not as easy as putting a smile on your face and asking caregivers to do the same. It includes creating an effective system that can be copied and repeated from place to place. I'll talk about how to set up the right culture in the following chapter.

CHAPTER 8

———

A Caring, Positive Culture: The Key to Success

Let me walk you through an episode I had while overseeing one of my residential care homes. The experience is not an isolated event; it is a situation I have been through many times during my years of operating residential care facilities. It begins in one of these homes, with an elderly gentleman whom we'll call Ed. Now, Ed had dementia, and his care plan was completely laid out to help him get through each day, cope with his ailments, and appreciate this stage of life.

One afternoon, Ed started feeling not so great. His symptoms deteriorated and developed into a serious problem. He had to relieve himself, but his body couldn't. Long story short, Ed needed a catheter. When something like this happens, the best thing to do is get to the hospital to get the problem fixed ASAP.

I knew this, and I also knew who would be accompanying Ed to the ER: me. There was no way I would send Ed off in an ambulance to the hospital and cross my fingers, hoping for the best. In my homes, a caregiver always goes with a resident to a medical appointment. In this case, it was of utmost importance that I go with Ed. Due to his dementia, it would be difficult for him to communicate with the doctors. He might not be able to explain his current symptoms, remember his other medical conditions, or list the medications he takes every day. But I could. I would be able to share details about his current and past health situations, along with the prescriptions he was regularly given. This might seem like a logical, straightforward process: We would go to the hospital, I would tell the medical team what was wrong, Ed would get treated, and we would go home. But I have been inside hospitals many times before (both as an employee and as a caregiver) and knew the system wasn't so simple.

As it turned out, I spent hours at the ER with Ed, working to get him the treatment he needed. During that time, if I had to leave for something else, another caregiver would come and stay at the hospital with Ed in my place. Together, we worked as advocates for Ed and his health. In the end, he got a catheter and was able to return to the residential care home, and I finally dropped into bed at 4:30 a.m.

I don't tell this story to pat myself on the back or let you know Ed's positive outcome; I mention it because it is one of the strategies that I have incorporated into the culture within residential care homes that follow my business model. In these places, providers and caregivers live and breathe for the well-being of our residents, and this plays out in numerous ways, including accompanying them on visits to the doctor or hospital.

Regardless of the way you set up a residential care home, to make it shine you'll need a culture in place that puts seniors first. I have not only developed a positive, caring culture within my residential care homes but also created an approach that has been placed in a uniform way into other homes. It all starts with hiring the best people, training them, and instilling a set of values that everyone can latch on to and hold up. I'll explain exactly how this is all done in the following sections.

A PERSONALIZED HIRING PROCESS

Go online to a job board and search for "caregiver." You'll generally find a long list of results. (A quick search on ZipRecruiter for the Seattle area yielded more than 150 options.) These are companies, and occasionally individuals, looking for workers to fill their caregiving positions.

If you are one of those companies looking for a caregiver, putting out an ad on one of these job boards can bring you calls for days—even weeks. But how can you find the right person? It takes hours to sift through the possibilities, and even then, you don't really know who you are getting.

I'll tell you how I have hired caregivers, and it's not typically through online job boards. In my practice, I would rarely post vacancies online. That's not because I think there is something wrong with it or distrust the individuals who are applying through the internet. The reason is simply that I really didn't need to use them. I usually have had enough contacts within my circle of acquaintances and referrals to fill the positions. When I first started my residential care home business, I asked others I knew from my past experiences working in the senior care industry to consider joining my staff in one of my homes. Over the years, I've built up a network of caregivers and acquaintances in the care industry. This means that when a position is open, it's generally been pretty easy for me to get a list of possible replacements.

Since the caregivers who have worked for me know my business model and understand my expectations, they have been careful when sharing referrals with me. They have recommended individuals they believe will be responsible and help run the business the way I like it. Due to this informed network, when I would make a new hire, the vast majority of the time they would be a good fit.

During the interview process, it's very important to listen to what the candidate says. Since I worked as a caregiver myself, I have a very good idea of the profile I want. Over my more than twenty years of experience, I've seen many caregivers with different personalities and approaches. By hearing how someone talks about senior care, I can usually identify if they will be a good match for a home that follows my business model.

In addition, I have a strong intuitive ability to really see inside an individual. Given this, when carrying out an interview, I ask a lot of questions and don't necessarily stick to the general ones like "Why do you want the job?" I know that these types of inquiries will usually attract generic, ill-defined responses like "This seems like a good place to work" or "I enjoy working with seniors." Those are fine answers, but I'm interested in more.

During conversations with a potential hire, I've gone over scenarios and asked the individual what they would do. In fact, during the interview, 80 percent of my questions have been based on examples. I might say, "We have a resident, and according to the care plan, she can be served fruit at breakfast every day. So you, as her caregiver, set out a plate of strawberries for her on a Monday morning. She doesn't complain, but she refuses to eat the food. What would you do?"

This is a very relevant question—the response that an individual gives would tell me many things about that person and their caregiving style. Suppose the candidate says, "Well, the resident has fruit in the care plan, so I would just try serving strawberries the next day again." From that answer, I can see where their focus is: on the details and care plan. Perhaps, instead, the interviewee says, "From my perspective, it's not like medication, which of course we have to be very strict about. I might ask if she wants a different kind of fruit, or if she isn't feeling well. I would try to find out why she isn't eating." That type of response shows me the caregiver is very concerned about the well-being of the resident. I've also heard answers such as "I would ask the supervisor what to do. I would explain that fruit is in the care plan and the resident didn't eat it.

I would suggest we monitor her food intake for the rest of the day too."
For me, answers such as these last two show that the individual is taking time to think through the situation and explore possible solutions.
It also indicates they view the resident as a human being and not some
object that needs to be cared for. They also are more concerned about
the resident's well-being than getting through tasks and checking boxes.

My process for the interview is one that I have developed through
my time in the industry, along with some trial and error. At first, when
I hired individuals for my residential care business, I often focused on
experience. If someone had all the certifications needed and ten years of
experience caring for seniors, I might hire them on the spot. "Wow," I
would think, "this person must really know what they are doing."

Not necessarily, I soon learned. Through experience, I came to realize that there are caregivers who certainly have ample experience but
lack something more important. They don't share the passion that I have
for caring for the elderly. To me, that passion is essential. It's a game
changer and absolutely necessary to successfully operate a residential
care home. Without it, the level of care will drop and the residents will
not be as satisfied as they could be.

For this reason, hearing that someone has passion has been a top
priority for me when conducting an interview. I have needed to learn
if the person has a deep longing in their core to do good things for the
elderly. I could train someone who has less experience but a heart full of
passion. And I have done this many times in my residential care homes.
What I've found is that some of the individuals with a strong desire to
care for the elderly who came under my training really grew and developed. Eventually they turned into the best of the best, the cream of the
crop in senior care. This, of course, is an all-around win: the caregiver is
happy and thrives, the residents adore the caregiver, and the residential
care business functions at a very high level.

THE ESSENTIAL TRAINING TIME

After I've hired an individual to work in one of my homes, I don't just tell them what to do. Instead, I personally show them how I run the home and how I like things done. If the new hire doesn't have a lot of experience, the orientation process needs to go incredibly in-depth. I've used it as an opportunity to help them dive into the care industry in general and really learn about the field. I have also shared my own secrets of the trade. If the worker has ample experience, we might breeze over certain basics, but I make sure to explain the way my homes are run so they can get up to speed with my expectations and the work environment.

Over the years of running my own homes, I have found this hands-on orientation process to be extremely effective. It has allowed me to demonstrate, in a detailed fashion, how I want residents to be cared for. We've gone through the logistics of giving medications, charting, tending to their activities, and making sure the resident is eating and getting healthy meals.

I have also shown how the other parts of the home operate. For example, I have gone into the kitchen and cooked. While standing at the stove, I might talk to the new caregiver about my beliefs and values when it comes to good nutrition. I might walk the caregiver through the garden, have them help me pick some green beans and squash, and then cook up the vegetables for the residents. Along with soups and salads, I've shown caregivers how to make smoothies and other drinks.

I've even partaken in the cleaning of the home. While doing this, I've worn the standard uniform of green scrubs, white socks, and white tennis shoes. I've run the vacuum, shined the sink—everything. I've been very matter-of-fact as I go about these chores and show the caregiver, step-by-step, what to look out for and what to remember with each task.

This training doesn't overlook the vital skills of communication with all kinds of individuals. You'll recall in previous chapters that I mentioned a residential care home is often buzzing with the activity of many people: residents are eating, playing a game, or tending to the garden; service providers are coming in to give therapies or haircuts; families are stopping by to pay a visit or discuss a change in a care plan.

A worker might shadow me for a day to see how communication can best be handled with these different groups. For instance, let's say I'm in a home with a new caregiver. It's midmorning on a weekday, at a time when a salon professional routinely shows up to do hair and nails. We smile and greet her, welcome her into the home, and check the schedule to see who has appointments for that day. Fifteen minutes later, a truck drives up with a bed full of plants. They have arrived to put in some new landscaping. We need to talk to the worker who brought the plants about where they should go. We ask for his recommendations and talk about next steps for the landscaping project. Then another car drives up. It's the daughter of one of the residents. She called earlier today and said she would stop by. Now she walks up to the home too. We step away from the landscaping and open the door for the daughter. When we ask her where she would like to talk to her father, she asks for a nice quiet space, which we quickly arrange. We bring out her father and ask if they'd like anything to eat or drink while they have a conversation. We make sure they are separated enough from the other residents so they can have a private discussion without getting interrupted.

See the picture I'm painting here? The scene accurately depicts what a typical residential care home might look like, in terms of people and the comings and goings, on a regular day. All staff members need to have great people skills! And while many who start working under my business model do have strong social abilities, it helps to show them how to listen to people coming through the house. It is also valuable for them to see how to handle issues and resolve minor conflicts before they get out of hand.

As well as focusing on great speaking and listening skills, I have helped staff members understand the way to handle doctor's appointments. I stated earlier that residents are always accompanied when they go to the doctor or hospital, but it's not a best practice to send new, inexperienced caregivers with the residents. They need to be aware of each resident's medical history and current health conditions.

When training new caregivers, I have always explained that senior's condition is often unique and complex and needs to be fully understood. Maybe they just had a stroke. Maybe they broke their hip and have to deal with pain every day as they recover. Perhaps they're in the early stages of dementia. Or they have diabetes and need to eat a very specific diet and take medications every day. Almost all residents, in fact, are going to need to take medicine every day. And they will probably have regular doctor's visits. They might need to go to the hospital or have a nurse regularly come in and see them.

Considering all these factors, it's essential to monitor their health conditions and be able to communicate to other professionals if and how they change. The lives of seniors aren't completely rosy every day, just as you and I don't live in a picture-perfect world. It's the reality of the senior experience. Thus I have shown staff how to be aware of changes, what needs to be done in an emergency, how to relate messages to doctors in a way that promotes action, and so on. I have told new caregivers that I don't find a 3:00 a.m. trip to the emergency room to be a bother, even if just precautionary, and especially if it is needed to help a senior get the right kind of care in that moment.

I feel strongly about a very hands-on orientation. It's important to me that staff members never see me as an unapproachable, removed authority figure. I haven't been a manager who comes in occasionally, walking through the home all dressed up and in heels. I haven't waltzed around a bit and then dictated orders while everyone else did the grunt work. I've worn the uniform, gotten on my hands and knees, and dug into the nitty-gritty everyday stuff. And I've loved every part of it.

When taking this approach, I have realized that caregivers will see me more as a team member than a manager. And that's exactly what I want. It means they're more likely to be up-front and open with me, honest about what's going on in the home, and willing to pitch in and do their part.

The training doesn't end after the initial orientation process. After hiring an individual and showing them how to do things in a way that follows my care model, I continue to be involved. I have had regular meetings with caregivers, and during these I have gone over any issues and also encouraged them about the important work they're doing. I have reminded them that I want them to treat each resident like they would their own mom or dad. There are so many ways we can help seniors enjoy this stage of their life. I have said things like "You are part of their final chapter, so look for ways to increase their happiness. Help them to be content and look after them as you would your own family members."

I have also used paychecks as a chance to talk about hard work and rewards. I might tell workers during a regular meeting, "Think about doing the right thing. When you hold that paycheck in your hand at the end of the month, ask yourself, 'Did I do everything right to get this check?' If you did everything right, you'll feel good about it." These are just some of the many ways I try to help ensure there is a positive, caring culture at all times. It doesn't work to simply tell workers to be positive and caring, though. They don't learn that way. Instead, they learn through seeing examples of tasks being executed well during their orientation and then receiving gentle reminders about giving top-notch care during regular meetings.

Now, drawing on my years of experience, I provide the instructions that other providers need to run the homes well. I share what has worked for me and explain why it is important to set an example. As providers follow my directions, they can watch their care homes perform well and run smoothly.

A CHANCE TO GROW

Just like the seniors in my residential care homes, caregivers tend to thrive in my employment. That's not a coincidence. I have worked hard to take good care of my staff; it's similar to my passion for senior care. I know deep in my core that caregivers need certain things to stay motivated. After making sure to hire someone with the required certifications and passion, and spending time training them and reinforcing a value system, we need to go one step further.

I love to walk into a home that sparkles from being cleaned thoroughly. I also appreciate seeing delicious, nutritious food being made in the kitchen. My heart is glad when I hear the happy sounds of conversation coming from the living room. If I enter one of my residential care homes that follows my philosophies and see outstanding performance, I'll be thrilled and won't hide my enthusiasm.

During my days of overseeing senior homes, it hasn't been uncommon for me to show up, take note of a great situation, and reward what I see. For instance, if I witness a caregiver working really hard to prepare healthy food in the kitchen, I might spontaneously give the worker a bonus. If I spot a staff member going above and beyond to make a resident comfortable, I'll often reward them with some extra money too.

This arrangement has several benefits. It encourages staff members to do their best. It also motivates them to make sure the house is presentable at all times. Furthermore, it assures them that their good work won't go unnoticed.

I have also treated workers well right from the start. Besides earning occasional bonuses, caregivers in my model enter a benefits system that provides paid vacation and pay raises. These two perks are significant, as you'll find that other residential care homes aren't quick to offer them. My plan does because I know the staff will operate better when they are well balanced by taking some vacation time and know there is a possibility to earn more through pay raises and bonuses.

I believe that encouragement doesn't end there. I have also created a way for caregivers to grow and develop in their own careers. I know that the right motivation can help a person move up in terms of responsibility and compensation. Given this, I've made it possible for workers to climb a ladder to step up to the next levels of caregiving.

Let's walk through an example to see how this is carried out. Say I hire a caregiver who starts with a base wage. The worker does a good job right from the start. After a little while working in my homes, the individual starts receiving occasional sporadic bonuses and also regular pay raises. Over time, I see that the individual is going the extra mile consistently. I might offer to make the caregiver a supervisor in one of my homes. This means a higher wage and also some more responsibility. They start to get involved in the logistics of the home's operations and see more of the behind-the-scenes tasks, which might include planning menus, ordering supplies, and organizing delivery schedules. Beyond that, I eventually position the best of the best for an incredible opportunity: they have the chance to become a provider themselves. This means they can oversee a residential care home on their own and even invest in the business. While doing this, they can still remain in my system to a certain extent. We can form a business partnership, and they have access to all my resources and programs. They implement the same best practices and caring culture. By staying under my umbrella, they can expect their home to perform well in the market and achieve a high cash flow.

And while I tend to keep bonuses sporadic to encourage hard work and motivate employees, I don't hide this ladder to success. New hires know right away that by coming into my business model, they are entering a world where they can grow personally and professionally. At the beginning, the steps can be laid out, and workers can see for themselves other caregivers stepping up in the system. My setup creates a snowball effect: others witness what's happening and want to jump on board, and there is more motivation all around.

Sound pretty great? It is. It's also something that you'll rarely find in other residential care homes. Many places are looking for ways to keep costs down and don't want to take on extra work such as a thorough orientation process, regular bonuses, paid vacation, and pay raises. In the short run, this might save a few dollars. But the cost-reducing measures could lead to a culture that gets hung up on expenses and cutting corners instead of providing great care.

Think of the impact of a vacancy for a moment. If you're charging residents $7,000 a month and have a house ready for six residents, one vacancy means the place brings in $7,000 less each month. Two vacancies would be a $14,000 shortage every month. Could you afford to keep a place running with that much of an income drop? Few places can manage vacancies for extended periods. That's why I have focused on avoiding those empty beds. By keeping employees motivated and well compensated, the home succeeds as a business. My model might require higher wages and bonuses than other places, but it also helps to avoid the heavy hit that can come from vacancies.

CREATING A REPEATABLE CULTURE

While I started with just a single residential care home, I have built up my business over the years. I have overseen multiple facilities, and earlier in this book I covered how operations can be streamlined throughout them all. It is definitely something that can help a business to grow. In addition to menus, compensation plans, and worker guidelines, other aspects can be strategized and made consistent in the homes. One key component is establishing the same culture in every home.

My business model outlines several methods that lead to a cultural standard in each home. One way this is done is through the staff. Since I oversee multiple homes, I have made sure all team members have enough hours and are treated well.

Say a worker starts off working twenty hours a week, but after a while, they ask for more time. It may not be possible to give them more time in their current home. Through my system, there could be connections that provide five extra hours every week in a different residence nearby.

You don't always see this shifting of workers in different residential care homes. Many operate as single operations and just can't give caregivers another place to work because it doesn't exist. Other owners have multiple residential care homes, but the atmosphere differs greatly between them. There is little mixing, and caregivers are offered a certain number of hours each week at just a single residence.

In homes that follow my design, as caregivers shift from place to place, they remain under my overarching residential care business and bring their training with them. They know that the care expectations for each home are the same. All the homes operate under the same brand. They always emphasize the need to put the seniors first and establish personal relationships with the residents.

When caregiving consistency is lacking, you'll often see it in the way that the elderly act in their homes. They might not feel a sense of routine, and, for example, their eating preferences could go unnoticed. Caregivers who come in and out of places may be unaware of each senior's habits and nuances. That's why I underscore the importance of continuity; after all, it's how relationships are built and often leads to improved health outcomes.

If a caregiver moves up the ladder and takes on a role as a provider, the benefits for a standardized culture continue. The person has undergone training and supervision already for a certain time. They understand the values to display, and already know many of the caregivers in the various homes and have working relationships with them.

It may be hard to see the immediate benefit from this streamlined culture, but I want to share here that my setup is not the norm. All too often, I have had owners of other residential care homes approach me. "How do you encourage your caregivers to stay?" they have asked. They might feel overwhelmed by the ongoing process of hiring individuals, watching them leave, and then having to go back to the starting line and look for another worker. They have become so consumed by maintaining a workforce in a single home that they haven't had the bandwidth to expand and branch out with additional enterprises. I point out to them the cost savings that come from maintaining a strong culture. In addition to lower resident vacancies, homes under my business umbrella have lower turnover rates for staff. Since caregivers are the frontline workers and the true face of the business, this is a big deal. It means residents can come to know and rely on steady caregivers. It means caregivers are happier and more willing to give their best efforts. Having a standard in place also makes it easier to establish the same expectations in every home. A repeatable culture that creates both satisfied residents and satisfied caregivers is a strong supporting block for a successful residential care home.

CARING FOR THE CAREGIVER

It would be remiss of me to talk about how well I have treated my caregivers and not cover some of the specific challenges they face regularly. Caregiving in any situation is incredibly demanding. Looking at the topic as a whole for a moment, we can see that more than forty million

Americans help care for an elderly family member.[72] (Here I'm referring to caregiving in the informal sense, as in an adult child helping out
their aging parent. I'm not talking about professional caregivers, though
I'll get to them in just a minute.) These informal assistants frequently
report an increase in emotional and physical strain. It's common for
family caregivers to feel constant stress and even to burn out. Some of
their symptoms include fatigue, depression, and a sense of being overwhelmed. In severe cases, the demands of caregiving can lead individuals to abuse alcohol or drugs.[73] In other words, it's a high-stress activity.

Even though I have hired caregivers who share my same passion, I
am also aware of the difficulties they face. Every day they may be dealing
with someone in the late stages of dementia who doesn't always know
where they are or throws fits and refuses to settle down. The caregiver
may listen to the same story told day after day or hear complaints about
how family members don't visit often enough. Residents in mental decline may even say harsh things to a caregiver or become aggressive, unaware of their surroundings and setting.

It's tough work, but that's why many of the practices I have implemented in my homes have made such a difference. Caregivers prefer to
stay at a job where they feel valued and cared for. It is easier for them if
they know they will be appreciated and compensated well for their efforts. Caregivers also often want to manage their stress so they can grow
in their profession. This desire works well with my business model.

The tendency for caregivers to suffer burnout is one of the reasons
I have offered paid vacation. I know that all workers need rest and time
away from the job. Helping team members support their own well-being
enables them to maintain energy while at work. They don't have to sacrifice a paycheck for rest, and that has made a difference, as many will stay
for years if they have a good balance between work and life.

There are other small details that help support caregivers. Keeping
the home drama-free goes a long way. One of the quickest ways to

provoke a caregiver to quit is by allowing family conflict into the home. As stated earlier, I have worked with residents' families to keep any issues they have outside their loved ones' living quarters. Also, making sure that the home is well stocked, schedules are followed, and the physical environment is maintained helps alleviate overall stress. And creating a welcoming space for residents is just as beneficial to caregivers; they are more likely to stay on in a home if they know the provider is doing everything possible to uphold a peaceful environment.

I should note that my experiences with caregivers in the past has not always played out perfectly. Life is a learning journey, and the path is often full of bumps. While I have had to let caregivers go on occasion, it's always been my preference to do everything I can to help them remain. I have always laid out expectations when hiring a worker, but if someone doesn't follow them, there are consequences. This is true for any line of work, but I mention it here to be completely transparent.

To sum up, a positive, caring culture keeps the needs of the residents and the caregivers in mind at all times. Residents will stay safe, content, and well cared for, while caregivers will appreciate their working environment, which encourages them to move forward in their careers. Done successfully, a consistent culture can be instilled and maintained in various homes for the long term. The processes are streamlined, workers know what to do and how to do it, they can shift from place to place, and turnover remains low all around.

The last two chapters have laid out the practices I've established to ensure a high cash flow in residential care homes. While these guidelines can help create a lucrative business, they have also taught me some lessons along the way. In the following chapter, I'll share some of the key takeaways that I've gleaned over the last two decades. Once you understand them, you'll be ready to get involved in the residential care home field, by investing, by working as a provider, or by playing the role of a caregiver.

CHAPTER 9

Putting It All Together

In the previous chapters, I've spent considerable time going over the history of residential care homes and their development. I've discussed my own background and how I fine-tuned a care model that puts seniors first. In fact, while I was putting this book together, I had to pause on several occasions to tend to my eldercare business. I happily dedicated hours for them because I know how important it is to care for the elderly, regardless of what time of day (or night!) it is. This is really what drives me to carry out my role in this industry, and it's why I ultimately have created this book to share.

In these last pages, I think we'll find value in reviewing the material covered in the previous chapters. I'll also spend some time observing the residential care industry and how it has changed in recent years, as well as where I see it heading. I'll share some of the lessons and takeaways I've gathered from working in this field. Lastly, we'll consider the difference that having a great partner (me!) can make, and what you can do for the next steps to really make an impact and help seniors.

A REVIEW OF RESIDENTIAL CARE HOMES

At the beginning of this book, I talked about how the elderly have always been an important part of my life, starting with the way I would care for my grandmom. I've spent decades—a lifetime, really—working with seniors, and this experience has given me the insight to take what I know works and put it into action.

Over the years, I have watched trends in senior care, and I know that among the elderly today, most want to stay home and age in place. However, there usually comes a point in time when they need more help with their daily activities. At that moment, they have several options available, including moving to an assisted-living facility, a nursing home, a continuing-care retirement community, or a memory-care facility. All these tend to have a limited number of caregivers overseeing many seniors at once—there are simply larger numbers involved, which sadly could make it more difficult for an elderly person to adapt in some cases and get personalized care.

There is another option for families and loved ones to consider, and this involves the residential care home. These places have an appeal for those looking for personal, customized care. This type of senior home tends to be located in a residential neighborhood and caters to individuals and families who can pay for either private care or Medicaid rates. For the purpose of this book, I have focused on private care. These residential homes have increased in popularity in recent years, especially with the pandemic and an interest among family members in having their loved ones receive personalized care.

There are opportunities related to residential care homes that can benefit others too, including investors who are looking for a way to make an impact and play a role in caring for America's aging segment. While there are many options for real estate investments, not all of them have long-term high cash flows. Residential care homes offer benefits that go beyond onetime opportunities like fix-and-flip projects. They are non-cyclical, as residents need care year-round and their families are often willing to maintain a long-term commitment.

For those looking to get involved in residential care homes, there are several approaches to take. You could opt to do everything on your own, and this method is often referred to as DIY investing. It involves an incredible amount of work and has many risks involved, especially for those who don't have experience in all the key areas, including but not limited to medical care, construction, managing, caregiving, business operating, licensing, and dealing with family relationships. Fortunately, there is another path that investors can choose, and this is to work with a partner who has the needed expertise. Those who have a professional background in real estate, such as real estate agents, might want to do part of the project on their own and bring in help for the rest. This is often where I come in, as I can make arrangements to fit specific needs ranging from assistance with a few tasks to in-depth planning and consulting.

I have the necessary skills and background to bring incredible value to any partnership, and this stems from my extensive network in all aspects of the industry. I have done everything from overseeing home remodeling and construction to getting the initial licenses and hiring caregivers, along with all the other things that are needed to make these homes work! Trust me, the list goes on and on—this is a complex space, and it should be, because seniors' lives are involved, and providing a space where they can thrive will always be the number one priority for me.

When working with me as a partner, it can be easier to set up some of the essential aspects I laid out in the previous chapters to hit a home run in this business. These include implementing best practices, and all best practices in my mind start with providing high-quality care. It's also important to create and maintain a brand to make the home stand out and to keep a positive environment and culture, as that can help make it easier for seniors to really feel comfortable. Another best practice for a high-cash-flow home involves smoothly managing relationships with family members, and even though this can be complicated, it's a necessary step to help seniors live in a peaceful environment.

In addition to benefits for investors, well-run residential care homes provide advantages for providers and caregivers. One of the ways in which everyone wins involves a well-planned, senior-first culture, and this begins with the right hiring practices. When caregivers are onboarded, they need proper training, and the instruction given should be consistent among workers. A great culture has opportunities for providers and caregivers to continue to grow. For instance, providers can consider running an additional home after they gain experience. Caregivers might accept more responsibilities, get extra hours, or even run their own home eventually. Taking measures to ensure staff members are well supported can go a long way and reduce turnover too.

As I've mentioned throughout the chapters, I have ample experience in everything that surrounds residential care homes. While I have loved setting up my own homes, I also thoroughly enjoy helping others learn strategies so they can succeed in this industry. I can draw on my extensive network to present opportunities and make connections at every level, from property acquisition to building, licensing, hiring practices, effective marketing, and home management.

INDUSTRY DEVELOPMENTS

I don't expect my passion for senior care to change. It has remained constant throughout my life, beginning with my earlier years. When I spent time caring for my grandmom, the seeds of a caring nature were planted in my heart. Moving away from Kenya to the United States instilled these tendencies more deeply, when I worked hard to earn my wages, start a life, and get to know the residents I was caring for. The passion has grown even further since I started my own residential care homes and developed the business model I've discussed in this book. It's what gets me out of bed in the morning, leads me to respond to urgent calls in the middle of the night, and helps me work around the clock to ensure the well-being of the seniors in my homes.

While that fundamental drive hasn't changed for me, residential care as an industry has really evolved. Caregiving as a practice has been around for some time (especially in the informal sense, as family members have historically found ways to care for the elderly). I've been involved in this segment for around two decades. As I saw changes in the care industry, I adjusted my own business model so I could continue operating my residential care homes successfully.

To help you see where the residential care home segment is today and where it is headed in the future, it's important to recognize some of the ways it has evolved. Doing so can help you make your own personal decisions when it comes to investing in this space. I know how to adapt as this industry changes and come out ahead. Let's look at some of the main shifts in the next sections.

Licensing Requirements

Occasionally, I've referred to licenses throughout this book, but I want to add here that the requirements for the industry have changed substantially in recent times. When I first started out, owning a residential care home was a relatively small business opportunity. If a person wanted to start their own residential care home, the process was comparatively easy. The costs were very low, as you simply had to make a home suitable for elderly residents and then open it for business. There weren't as many licensing requirements or regulations to follow as there are today.

During this time, some residential care homes, like mine, did well.

Others managed to stay open but didn't really grow or make much of an income. A few failed quickly and had to close their doors. This period was a learning experience for everyone.

As time went on, the residential care home segment responded to the growing number of aging citizens throughout the country. More baby boomers were retiring, living on their own, and then needing a different place to stay. Their families were more often saying no to nursing homes and assisted-living facilities. They wanted something that felt more personal and didn't involve such a high number of residents living in a single building. They searched for an option that seemed more homelike, one that appeared akin to what the aging senior had been living in their whole life.

In the state of Washington, for example, more residential care homes opened in response to this demand. During this time, there were new licensing requirements added to the process of setting up and running a home. My residential care home business, along with others in the industry, was about to face a significant change.

We had to follow more regulations to maintain all the proper licenses. For me, this wasn't too difficult. I had already set up a place that was in great condition. I was already knee-deep in the process of forming the best practices and business model I described earlier in the book. Having always focused on high-quality care and providing a lot of amenities, I didn't have to undergo large remodels or installations to meet new codes. Some homes, like mine, adapted and followed the rules. Others didn't abide by the newer regulations and faced steep fines or had to close.

Change Brings Opportunities

Regulations regarding the number of homes an individual can operate have shifted as well. For a while, in the state of Washington, those of us in the residential care home market were only allowed to run one home if we had no licensing history. That changed too—after a year in good standing, we were given permission to open second homes. After three years of very good standing, we could become multiproviders, meaning we could run several homes at a time.

While every state is different, in Washington this presented a wonderful business opportunity. As I looked at the laws and considered my own business, I realized there could be a way for me to make a bigger impact. Yes, I loved helping the individuals in my home, but I knew it would be even better if I could do more. What if the model I had built up over time could be replicated in many homes? What if by expanding, I could allow more seniors to experience happy moments and more caregivers to work in a place that looked out for them? I knew I already had a system in place that was successful; now, by branching out, I could help society even more.

Furthermore, this opportunity gave others a chance to get involved. Investors could come in and play a role. They would be able to help support the senior segment in society. They would also be able to reap high returns, provided they invested through the model I developed.

Providers and caregivers would be able to participate in my systems too. They could fulfill their dream of running their own home or working in a place where they could really help seniors enjoy life. These workers would appreciate the financial and emotional benefits that come from being in a great environment with the training I could offer.

Even as I was thinking about expanding, I needed to be realistic about how the industry had evolved. Along with the boom among residential care homes, the playing field changed. By that, I mean the competition grew tougher—much tougher.

Today, there are many residential care homes on the scene, making it much more difficult to operate with ineffective branding and marketing. Everyone in the business has had to do something more. They've needed to position themselves in a specific way to attract families. In other words, residential care homes must have a niche within the market. If they don't, families might not fully understand what they offer and will be drawn to a place that clearly defines what their aging parent will receive.

Search for a residential care home online, and you'll see that establishments all over have responded to the increased competition. You'll find small, traditional homes that specialize in low-end accommodations and have lower rates; you'll see expansive properties with luxurious interiors that cater to ultrawealthy clientele and charge higher rates; and so on. Residential care homes have identified their target audience and set up shop to serve those specific needs. Like many other industries, the residential care home segment has grown, developed, and branched out into different subsegments.

LOOKING AHEAD

We've covered the history of residential care homes and discussed the trends of today, but what about the future? How can we be sure the residential care home boom will continue? Are there signs indicating that the market is getting too saturated and doesn't warrant an investment?

One clear indicator that residential care homes have a solid place in the real estate scene lies in the statistics. In the United States, there were fifty-four million people aged sixty-five and older in 2020.[74] The number of seniors is expected to hit seventy-two million by 2030.[75] Moving forward to 2050, the senior population is predicted to reach eighty-three million.[76] Many of those millions of people will need more care at a certain point.

As we've seen, some families are searching for a more personal setting for their aging relative. There are signs that this tendency will continue. First and foremost, the concept of wanting a customized experience aligns with current consumer preferences. To see this connection, consider the movements we've witnessed in industries such as entertainment and information. Television sets began to be sold to the American public in 1939; they were black-and-white. Individuals who lived during the 1950s and 1960s may recall television sets—and color—entering their living rooms.[77] Back then, there were few channels and limited options for viewing. A family might sit down on a Saturday night and watch a show together.

Now, we have a long list of devices that we can use to access entertainment and information. A family might still sit down on a Saturday night, but everyone has the option to stream the show of their choice on their individual device. If they decide to watch a show together, they will be bypassing a multitude of other entertainment selections that are just as available, including news stations, live-streaming options, and consumer-driven content like YouTube. The trend has created an expectation among consumers: we've grown accustomed to this availability and selection. If you were to ask everyone in a household if they would like to switch out all their devices, along with their cable and internet connections, for a black-and-white TV that offered just four programs a day at set times, it isn't hard to imagine their reactions.

Now, I ask you, if customers want this for their entertainment, how much more will they be interested in customized care for their dear grandmother? While information has become consumer-focused, there are many other segments adopting this approach. Both retail and service-oriented industries are shifting to a customer-first approach. The emphasis is on the client's taste, rather than on the company's product or offering. When it comes to residential care homes, I fully anticipate a growing desire for customization. When paying for a service, families are becoming used to being able to make specific requests and have their needs accounted for.

Given the increase in demand for personalization, residential care homes that have streamlined processes and best practices in place will do well. They will be able to maintain their current operations in an efficient way, which will allow them to focus on catering to each resident and family. On the flip side, DIY residential care homes may struggle. They might end up piling their efforts into the logistics of operating a home and leave little room to create further personalized experiences.

These shifts within the residential care home to more customizable experiences reflect paths that other industries have taken. Consider the case of Chipotle and the restaurant industry. Its founder, Steve Ells, graduated from the Culinary Institute of America and dreamed of starting a fine-dining restaurant. He didn't have the funds to immediately open a restaurant, so he went to work as a sous chef, where he fine-tuned his cooking skills and learned best practices. In 1993, he set out on his own and opened Chipotle with a $85,000 loan from his father. By then, his vision had evolved, and the restaurant produced fast food known for its quality and service. With its organic ingredient lineup and customizable options, Chipotle's fan base—and revenue—skyrocketed. Two years later, in 1995, Ells used cash generated from the original restaurant to open a second one. Soon more stores opened, and the chain started gaining traction.[78] In 2021, annual revenue surpassed $7.5 billion,[79] and by 2022, there were three thousand locations.[80] Customers were still lining up for the nutritious, made-for-you dining experience and menu that Ells featured in his original restaurant.

I believe the best opportunities for investors interested in the residential care home segment can be found in preexisting and proven models. Relying on a partner who knows the business and understands how to stand above the competition is the ticket to a high cash flow. Someone who has created a scalable plan can hold the keys to expansive, lucrative success. Just as Chipotle multiplied its operations to an eager market during the last decades, my residential care homes are designed to replicate and pop up around the country in a similar way.

MY TAKEAWAYS

Because I've been part of the senior care industry for so long, I've observed and adapted to changing environments. When governments added more regulations, I realized it was a necessary step. With more residential care homes, there was simply a greater need for rules to help ensure seniors could get the best care possible. In a field where, unfortunately, abuses can occur, I am completely in favor of doing everything we can to protect seniors.

I've also learned about senior care throughout my life and career. Whenever I have witnessed something that I thought could be improved, I have actively looked for ways to make changes where I could. This experience is really what has helped me figure out how to run a successful home myself. Now I am able to share my best strategies with others so they can reap the benefits and play an important role too.

One aspect of caregiving that I have always especially loved is the chance to get to know the senior. What were they like in their younger years? How do they prefer to start their day? What are their favorite memories? What activities provide them with a sense of fulfillment? By creating a model that focuses on personal relationships, I have set up a system where providers and caregivers can learn all sorts of details about the residents. This information can be used to create a routine that the senior loves and a daily structure that gives them a chance to thrive.

NEXT STEP: REACH OUT TO ME

If I could summarize my approach to senior care in one word, it would be "humanity." I look at seniors as individual human beings who need special treatment because of their particular stage in life. As you've seen in the previous pages, caring for seniors is not an easy job, but in the world that I have created, it is full of opportunities. I believe in taking the time to connect with older people and help them live their very best lives. I have spent countless hours developing strategies that enable them to optimally function and cope with their conditions. I have always placed people over tasks, and my model focuses on providing a high quality of life for all residents!

I love that we can do this for seniors. I've spent my entire life looking for ways to help people. When I see changes for the good, I know I am doing the right thing. It drives me to continue evolving and carrying out my passion and helping others through partnerships, connections, and referrals.

And now I invite you to join me in this effort to improve the senior-care system in our society. I want to give you the chance to make a difference in the lives of the elderly. Trust me when I say that older individuals won't be the only ones who are rewarded for your efforts. Their families will thank you, and you'll truly feel like you've had an impact on society.

The time to act is now. Seniors are aging as you read this. Most likely a family member, at this very moment, is searching the internet for a senior home. They might be typing in the words "home for mom" and finding thousands of results to sort through. These adult children aren't naive; they know better than to click on the first result they see. They're likely to read through reviews and tour potential homes before making a commitment.

Indeed, you can play a part in this important movement to help families who are searching for a residential care home where their loved one will be comfortable and content. You can be involved in some way to help build an outstanding culture where seniors thrive and the business does too. You could be a provider, welcoming in families and helping their loved ones get settled. You might be a caregiver, overseeing the daily activities of an elderly person in a positive environment.

For investors, by participating on the financial side, you can help these humane interactions with seniors take place more often and in more homes throughout America.

Come with me on the journey to create better days for seniors and their families! The first step doesn't have to be searching for the perfect property or trying out some of the best practices I've laid out on your own. It doesn't require heavily researching the construction methods to learn about home remodels. And it doesn't include touring every senior home in your area.

Instead, I encourage you to opt for the simple, straightforward approach. Reach out and contact me. I'm ready and eager to partner with you. Let's work together to make a difference!

Learn more at makingadifferencewithnelly.com.

NOTES

CHAPTER 1

1. "Ageing," United Nations, https://www.un.org/en/global-issues/ageing.
2. "Aging in Place: A State Survey of Livability Policies and Practices," National Conference of State Legislatures with the AARP Public Policy Institute, https://assets.aarp.org/rgcenter/ppi/liv-com/ib190.pdf.
3. "The United States of Aging Survey," AARP, https://www.aarp.org /content/dam/aarp/livable-communities/old-learn/research/the-united -states-of-aging-survey-2012-aarp.pdf.
4. "Long-Term Care Facilities: Assisted Living, Nursing Homes, and Other Residential Care," National Institute on Aging, https://www.nia.nih.gov /health/assisted-living-and-nursing-homes/long-term-care-facilities -assisted-living-nursing-homes.
5. "Cost of Care Survey," Genworth, https://www.genworth.com/aging -and-you/finances/cost-of-care.html.
6. "What Caregivers Should Know About Nursing Home Care," WebMD, https://www.webmd.com/health-insurance/nursing-home-care#1.
7. Joy Intriago, "Staff to Resident Ratio in Assisted Living Facilities," Seasons, https://www.seasons.com/staff-to-resident-ratio/2491965/.
8. "Nursing Homes," MedlinePlus, https://medlineplus.gov/nursinghomes .html#:~:text=Some%20nursing%20homes%20are%20set,to%20be%20 more%20like%20home.

9. "Custodial Care vs. Skilled Care," Centers for Medicare and Medicaid Services, https://www.cms.gov/Medicare-Medicaid-Coordination/Fraud-Prevention/Medicaid-Integrity-Education/Downloads/infograph-CustodialCarevsSkilledCare-%5BMarch-2016%5D.pdf.

10. "Nursing Homes," HealthinAging.org, https://www.healthinaging.org/age-friendly-healthcare-you/care-settings/nursing-homes.

11. "Cost of Care Survey," Genworth, https://www.genworth.com/aging-and-you/finances/cost-of-care.html.

12. "Nursing Homes," HealthinAging.org.

13. Jayme Kennedy, "The Pros and Cons of Continuing Care Retirement Communities," Care, https://www.care.com/c/stories/15232/continuing-care-retirement-community-pros-and-cons/.

14. "7 Senior Housing Options: Which Works Best?," DailyCaring, https://dailycaring.com/senior-housing-options-overview/.

CHAPTER 2

15. Names have been changed.

16. Maria Riedl, Franco Mantovan, and Christa Them, "Being a Nursing Home Resident: A Challenge to One's Identity," *Nursing Research and Practice*, https://www.hindawi.com/journals/nrp/2013/932381/.

17. Jules Rosen, "A Doctor's View: Depression in Long-Term Care Residents," *Health Progress*, https://www.chausa.org/publications/health-progress/article/november-december-2014/a-doctor%27s-view-depression-in-long-term-care-residents.

18. Rosen, "A Doctor's View: Depression in Long-Term Care Residents."

19. Rosen, "A Doctor's View: Depression in Long-Term Care Residents."

20. Rosen, "A Doctor's View: Depression in Long-Term Care Residents."

21. Gregg Girvan, "The COVID Nursing Home Crisis Was 50 Years in the Making," *The Dispatch*, https://thedispatch.com/article/the-covid-nursing-home-crisis-was/.

22. Karen Yourish, K. K. Rebecca Lai, Danielle Ivory, and Mitch Smith, "One-Third of All U.S. Coronavirus Deaths Are Nursing Home Residents," *New York Times*, https://www.nytimes.com/interactive/2020/05/09/us/coronavirus-cases-nursing-homes-us.html.

23. Lindsay Fendt, "As Coronavirus Slows Its Spread in Elder Care Homes, Residents Still Face Another Health Battle: Loneliness," *CPR News*, https://www.cpr.org/2020/06/10/as-coronavirus-slows-its-spread-in-elder-care-homes-residents-still-face-another-health-battle-loneliness/.

24. Fendt, "As Coronavirus Slows Its Spread in Elder Care Homes, Residents Still Face Another Health Battle: Loneliness."

25. Chris McGreal, "'We're Living in Fear': Why US Nursing Homes Became Incubators for the Coronavirus," https://www.theguardian.com/world/2020/apr/15/were-living-in-fear-why-us-nursing-homes-became-incubators-for-the-coronavirus.

26. "Covid-19," Adult Family Home Council, https://adultfamilyhomecouncil.org/covid-19/.

27. Names have been changed.

28. Sophie Quinton, "Staffing Nursing Homes Was Hard Before the Pandemic. Now It's Even Tougher," *Fierce Healthcare*, https://www.fiercehealthcare.com/hospitals-health-systems/staffing-nursing-homes-was-hard-before-pandemic-now-it-s-even-tougher.

29. Quinton, "Staffing Nursing Homes Was Hard Before the Pandemic. Now It's Even Tougher."

30. "Occupational Employment and Wage Statistics," https://www.bls.gov/oes/home.htm.

31. Quinton, "Staffing Nursing Homes Was Hard Before the Pandemic. Now It's Even Tougher."

CHAPTER 3

32. "Life Expectancy in the USA, 1900–98: Men and Women," Berkeley, https://u.demog.berkeley.edu/~andrew/1918/figure2.html.

33. "U.S. Life Expectancy 1950–2023," Macrotrends, https://www.macrotrends.net/countries/USA/united-states/life-expectancy#:~:text=The%20current%20life%20expectancy%20for,a%200.03%25%20decline%20from%202017.

34. "2019 Alzheimer's Disease Facts and Figures," Alzheimer's Association, https://www.alz.org/media/documents/alzheimers-facts-and-figures-2019-r.pdf.

35. "2019 Alzheimer's Disease Facts and Figures."

36. Eric C. Nordman, "The State of Long-Term Care Insurance: The Market, Challenges and Future Innovations," National Association of Insurance Commissioners and the Center for Insurance Policy and Research, https://content.naic.org/sites/default/files/inline-files/cipr_current_study_160519_ltc_insurance.pdf.

37. Nordman, "The State of Long-Term Care Insurance: The Market, Challenges and Future Innovations."

38. "What Are Nursing Homes/Skilled Nursing Facilities and How Much Should They Cost?" AssistedLiving.org, https://www.assistedliving.org /nursing-homes/.

39. "What Are Nursing Homes/Skilled Nursing Facilities and How Much Should They Cost?"

40. "Long-Term Care Providers and Services Users in the United States, 2015–2016," National Center for Health Statistics, U.S. Department of Health and Human Services, https://www.cdc.gov/nchs/data/series /sr_03/sr03_43-508.pdf.

41. "What Are Nursing Homes/Skilled Nursing Facilities and How Much Should They Cost?"

42. "What Are Nursing Homes/Skilled Nursing Facilities and How Much Should They Cost?"

43. Kathleen Gifford et al., "A View from the States: Key Medicaid Policy Changes: Results from a 50-State Medicaid Budget Survey for State Fiscal Years 2019 and 2020," KFF, https://www.kff.org/report-section/a -view-from-the-states-key-medicaid-policy-changes-long-term -services-and-supports/.

44. "Board and Care Homes," Encyclopedia.com, https://www.encyclopedia .com/medicine/psychology/psychology-and-psychiatry/group-homes.

45. Kelly Simon, "In Depth: A Crisis in Long-Term Care: Assisted Living Facilities, Nursing Homes Struggle to Find Workers," *Daily Citizen*, https://wiscnews.com/news/community/bdc/news/local/in-depth -a-crisis-in-long-term-care-assisted-living-facilities-nursing-homes -struggle-to/article_2b63cfe7-d32e-5ae8-ae7e-12b8bd2bdd38.html.

46. "Special Report: Investor Home Buying," CoreLogic, https://www .corelogic.com/intelligence/special-report-investor-home-buying/.

47. "America's Rental Housing 2022," Joint Center for Housing Studies of Harvard University, https://www.jchs.harvard.edu/sites/default/files /reports/files/Harvard_JCHS_Americas_Rental_Housing_2022.pdf

48. Valerie Kalfrin, "6 Types of Real Estate Investment You Should Know About," HomeLight, https://www.homelight.com/blog/types-of-real -estate-investments/.

49. Andrew Beattie, "5 Simple Ways to Invest in Real Estate," Investopedia, https://www.investopedia.com/investing/simple-ways-invest-real -estate/.

50. Arthur Colker, "The Ultimate List of Vacation Rental Statistics—2022," StayFi, https://stayfi.com/vrm-insider/2021/06/21/the-ultimate-list-of -vacation-rental-statistics-2020-edition/.

51. "Vacation Rental Market Size, Share and Trends Analysis Report by Booking Mode (Online, Offline), By Accommodation Type (Home, Resort/Condominium), By Region (Asia Pacific, North America), and Segment Forecasts, 2023–2030," Grand View Research, https://www.grandviewresearch.com/industry-analysis/vacation-rental-market#:~:text=The%20global%20vacation%20rental%20market%20size%20was%20estimated%20at%20USD,USD%2082.63%20billion%20in%202022.

52. Adam Grucela, "Vacation Rental: 100+ Statistics, Facts, and Trends [2023]," Passport-photo.online, https://passport-photo.online/blog/vacation-rental-industry-statistics/#:~:text=The%20vacation%20rental%20demand%20in,over%2Dyear%20(YoY).

53. "U.S. Home Flipping Returns Drop to Seven-Year Low in 2018," ATTOM, https://www.attomdata.com/news/most-recent/2018-year-end-u-s-home-flipping-report/.

CHAPTER 4

54. "Survival Rates and Firm Age," U.S. Small Business Administration Office of Advocacy, https://advocacy.sba.gov/2016/11/01/startup-rates-and-firm-age/.

55. "Survival Rates and Firm Age," U.S. Small Business Administration Office of Advocacy.

56. R. L. Adams, "10 Reasons Why 7 Out of 10 Businesses Fail Within 10 Years," *Entrepreneur*, https://www.entrepreneur.com/leadership/10-reasons-why-7-out-of-10-businesses-fail-within-10-years/299522.

57. Angela Chapa, "What Is a Sales Funnel, Examples and How to Create One," *Daily Egg*, https://www.crazyegg.com/blog/sales-funnel/.

58. R. L. Adams, "10 Reasons Why 7 Out of 10 Businesses Fail Within 10 Years."

59. George Meszaros, "50 Reasons Why Some Businesses Fail While Others Succeed," SuccessHarbor.com, https://www.successharbor.com/why-some-businesses-fail-while-others-succeed-02132015/.

CHAPTER 5

60. "What Qualifications Do I Need to Become an Adult Family Home Provider?" Washington State Department of Social and Health Services, https://www.dshs.wa.gov/node/30667.

61. "NHA License," Missouri Department of Health and Senior Services, https://health.mo.gov/information/boards/bnha/nhalicense.php#:~:text=A%20licensed%20nursing%20home%20administrator,examine%20or%20receive%20a%20license.

62. "What Is SEO—Search Engine Optimization?" Search Engine Land, https://searchengineland.com/guide/what-is-seo.

63. Name has been changed.

64. Karla T. Washington et al., "Family Perspectives on the Hospice Experience in Adult Family Homes," *Journal of Gerontological Social Work*, https://www.ncbi.nlm.nih.gov/pmc/articles/PMC3023972/.

65. Craig Sailor, "A Puyallup Group Home Left a 95-Year-Old Where She Fell. Ten Days Later, She Was Dead," *News Tribune*, https://www.thenewstribune.com/news/local/article240071173.html.

CHAPTER 6

66. Name has been changed.

67. Washington et al., "Family Perspectives on the Hospice Experience in Adult Family Homes," *Journal of Gerontological Social Work*.

CHAPTER 7

68. Catherine Hawes, "Elder Abuse in Residential Long-Term Care Settings: What Is Known and What Information Is Needed?," *Elder Mistreatment: Abuse, Neglect, and Exploitation in an Aging America*, https://www.ncbi.nlm.nih.gov/books/NBK98786/.

69. Hawes, "Elder Abuse in Residential Long-Term Care Settings: What Is Known and What Information Is Needed?"

70. Hawes, "Elder Abuse in Residential Long-Term Care Settings: What Is Known and What Information Is Needed?"

71. Michael J. Berens, "DSHS Seeks Crackdown on Adult Family Homes," *Seattle Times*, https://www.seattletimes.com/seattle-news/dshs-seeks-crackdown-on-adult-family-homes/.

CHAPTER 8

72. "2020 Report: Caregiving in the U.S.," AARP, https://www.aarp.org/content/dam/aarp/ppi/2020/05/full-report-caregiving-in-the-united-states.doi.10.26419-2Fppi.00103.001.pdf.

73. "Caregiver Stress: Tips for Taking Care of Yourself," Mayo Clinic, https://www.mayoclinic.org/healthy-lifestyle/stress-management/in -depth/caregiver-stress/art-20044784.

CHAPTER 9

74. "2020 Profile of Older Americans," Administration for Community Living, https://acl.gov/sites/default/files/aging%20and%20Disability %20In%20America/2020Profileolderamericans.final_.pdf.
75. Jennifer M. Ortman, Victoria A. Velkoff, and Howard Hogan, "An Aging Nation: The Older Population in the United States," United States Census Bureau, https://www.census.gov/content/dam/Census/library /publications/2014/demo/p25-1140.pdf.
76. Ortman et al., "An Aging Nation: The Older Population in the United States."
77. "When Was the First Black and White Television Set Invented?" *Reference*, https://www.reference.com/history-geography/first-black -white-television-invented-1f23b05c4a2fc1a.
78. "Chipotle Startup Story," Fundable, https://www.fundable.com/learn /startup-stories/chipotle.
79. "Chipotle Mexican Grill Revenue 2010–2023," Macrotrends, https://www.macrotrends.net/stocks/charts/CMG/chipotle-mexican -grill/revenue.
80. "All Chipotle Locations in the US," Chipotle, https://locations .chipotle.com/.

ACKNOWLEDGMENTS

———

My grandmother: for raising me with so much love! And for giving me the confidence to always believe in my dreams and the work ethic to achieve them!

My four amazing children: for inspiring me and motivating me in literally everything I do!

My husband: for all your endless support and unconditional love!

And above all, my God, who makes everything possible through Him!

ABOUT THE AUTHOR

Originally from Kenya, where she was raised by her grandmother, Nelly Some worked in tourism and women's rights as a young adult. After moving to the United States, she built up businesses and created successful investment models in the area of senior care.

Nelly spent more than two decades in the healthcare sector and has worked as a primary caregiver, emergency-room technician, and as the owner and manager of multiple residential care homes. She has extensive experience that spans more than twenty years in all the applicable settings surrounding elderly care, including buying, renovating, and managing private homes, as well as previously working in hospitals, nursing homes, and assisted-living facilities.

Over the years, Nelly has developed systems and cultures for residential care homes that help them stand out from others on the market. Her expertise in the areas of senior care management, real estate, and senior home renovating, coupled with a passion to make seniors' lives better, has enabled her to rise above others in this space. Drawing on this experience, she created a unique and successful residential care home model for investors and others to follow. Additionally, Nelly started her own complementary businesses as a real estate broker, contractor, and owner of a referral agency. She is the owner and designated broker of NESCO Realty Group and has bought and sold many residential care homes for herself and others.

Nelly attributes her success in this world to the love given to her by her grandmother. Now, her life's mission is to give back to other seniors like her grandmother.